TALES
FROM
ALBANIA

Mark D. Vickers

"Tales from Albania", written by Mark D. Vickers
Cover Design by Mayapur-sasi Dasa
Book Layout by Mayapur-sasi Dasa

ISBN:
First published in softback, December 2021.
Second published in hardback, October 2022.

Published by Besa.

DEDICATION

To the people of Albania who accepted me into their country, shared their hospitality, welcomed me into their homes, and inspired me to at least learn something of their culture and rich history.

ACKNOWLEDGMENTS

I would like to thank Edlira Babamusta-Gay who has been a wonderful friend since she first stepped into my classroom in 2004 to introduce me to the fascinating Albanian language. I have lived in four other countries since then, from Albania to Taiwan, but Edlira's friendship is as strong today as it ever was. Our families have remained in touch throughout all these years, and I cannot thank her enough.

I must also thank Edlira's sister, Dr. Ermira Babamusta, who has encouraged my writing of a number of articles about Albania over the years, and helped me see them published in Albania, USA, and Kosovo. I have always felt sincere gratitude for advice on such matters.

I wish to thank Mag. Dr. Joachim Matzinger, Research Fellow in Balkan Studies at the Institute for Habsburg and Balkan Studies at the Austrian Academy of Sciences, who gave me permission to quote freely from Robert Elsie's many wonderful books and website. Robert and I exchanged a number of emails before he passed away.

Finally, to Prof. Dr. (Profesor Emeritus) Refik Kadija, introduced to me by Edlira Babamusta-Gay, who gave me great encouragement after he read the English language version of this book, and agreed to translate it into Albanian.

CONTENTS

4   Dedication.

5   Acknowledgments.

7   About the Author.

9   Introduction.

30   First Encounters with Albania.

43   The Language Exam.

48   Peshkopi to Fushe Lure, via Gryke Nokë.

63   The Day of Our Lady of Shkodra.

69   Corfu to Gjirokaster via Saranda
       (including the Corfu Channel Incident).

87   The Bribe.

90   Berati with Arsi.

97   My Very Good Friend, Zoti Riza Lahi.

107 The Legend of Rozafa.

116 Kolë Idromeno.

122 O Moj Shqypni – poem by Pashko Vasa (including translation).

128 Ura E Mesit – The Mes Bridge, Near Shkodra.

134 The British in Albania During World War Two.

164 Edith Durham.

170 The Bridge (Traveling Alongside the River Mat).

187 A Collection of Old Magazine Illustrations About Albania.

199 Migjeni.

212 Colourful Kruja.

220 Ensnared by the Two-Headed Eagle.

240 Annex A: Books by Edith Durham.

241 Annex B: A Selection of Books by Robert Elsie.

242 Annex C: British Deaths in Albania in World War Two.

248 Bibliography.

ABOUT THE AUTHOR

Mark Vickers was born and raised in UK. When he was 16 he entered a school for potential army officers, and from there was accepted into the Royal Military Academy Sandhurst as an army officer cadet. Having received his commission as a Second Lieutenant he was posted to the Brigade of Gurkhas in Hong Kong, and spent the rest of his 33 year career in various countries around the world including three years in Albania.

In 2004 he was selected to be the British Defence Attaché to Albania between 2005 – 2008, a diplomatic post, which involved a year's preparation. This was the start of his deep interest in Albania and the Albanian people, way beyond that expected for professional necessity. This soon became a passion which has continued until today. He became especially fascinated by the history, traditions and culture. He often comments that his three years in Albania were the highlight of his career, not only from a work point of view, but also because of his enjoyment of this ancient country and its people.

In 2008 he moved from Albania to his next appointment in Nepal for three years, and thereafter to Afghanistan on an operational tour of duty, before taking early retirement and emigrating to Taiwan where he now spends time writing, painting, and religious studies and practice. Nevertheless, he has continued to maintain close and warm links with Albania, a place which remains more dear to his heart than anywhere else.

He has written a number of articles about the country which have been published in newspapers and magazines in Albania, Kosovo and New York.

In 2018 he very much hoped that he was returning to live and work in Albania. He would prefer not to say in which role, but at the 11th hour, sadly and without explanation, it all came to naught. His passion for this fascinating country continues.

INTRODUCTION

I regret never having kept a diary for the three years that I lived in Albania, and yet my many memories of those very happy times are clearer and multitudinous than for anywhere else I have ever lived. I can only surmise that this is a reflection of how deeply this small Balkan country called Albania, Shqipëria - the Land of the Eagles, has affected me and touched my heart.

Sometimes when reading a book we skip over the introduction, especially one as lengthy as this, but I encourage you to read this as it may answer a number of questions about what I have included, and what I have chosen to omit.

Since leaving Albania I have written a number of articles which have been printed in newspapers and magazines in Albania, Kosovo and New York, and read as far away as Australia, Turkey, Russia, and England. The feedback I received from these, especially from the Albanian diaspora, became the nucleus of an idea to create a book of short stories, some personal reminiscences, some historical, some folklore, a few light-hearted, and one or two hopefully thought-provoking. This is that book.

Through this book I hope to share with you some of my own passion for the wonderful and fascinating aspects of Albania and the Albanian people. It is not an attempt at a scholarly tome, but rather an accurate account of my own personal experiences, hopefully enhanced by recounting aspects of the country which have somehow inspired me or grabbed my attention. I am sure we have all been on guided tours where the tour guide spews forth fact after fact which they have memorized and now repeat in a monotone and disinterested voice. Some books are also like that. This is the opposite of what I am striving for in this modest volume. Rather than simply recounting all my various travels around the country I offer a varied range of topics in an attempt to illustrate the breadth and richness to be discovered. Included are stories of history, geography, folklore and personalities but hopefully conveyed in a manner which will leave you, dear reader, wanting to know more and delve deeper, not glad the "tour" is over!

I have included an overview of the amazing British woman, Edith Durham, who developed a love for the country and its people over 100 years ago. Her name remains well known in Albania even today. One personal indulgence is a chapter about the role of the British in Albania during the Second World War as depending on one's viewpoint this may be seen as something positive, neutral, or negative. But beyond the actual bravery of the individuals involved, I hope that in briefly telling this story it will explain something of the complicated situation amongst the different factions in Albania at that pivotal period of Albanian history, the sad result being over four decades of extreme communism and isolationism.

Albania is still a country of mystery and ancient traditions, some of which are hard to define or understand for anyone outside that culture, or perhaps I should more correctly say, cultures, as Albania has more than one. Albanians are well known, and rightly so, for showing the best hospitality to guests that one can find anywhere in the world, yet at the same time they may be less than forthcoming in opening up to strangers until trust is won. Perhaps this is as a result of the country having endured so many invasions over many centuries, followed by decades of communist repression during which one would always have had to remain cautious about saying anything to anyone. A shared history and culture shape us, and those decades of extreme communism have affected the identity of at least two, possibly three, generations. But this was not the first period of tribulation which this sturdy race has endured. Previously they have been pulled this way and that by Turk, Greek, Bulgarian, Italian, Serb, Russian, Austrian, and yet somehow through all this they have always emerged with their own distinctive culture in tact.

It is a small country, with more Albanians living outside its borders than within, and yet it is an extremely complex and fascinating place and race. I have so many memories and so many stories to tell, and the most difficult decision I faced in compiling this book has been whether to include the inevitable many stories and personalities connected to my work in Albania. I do not mean to suggest that my work itself was in any way "secret", it was not, and in any case I have deliberately waited this long to finish writing this book so that my work involvement is "time expired". After considerable consideration, I have decided not to talk about any of this but allow me to write a few sentences here. In some way, the following paragraphs are not simply about me but more importantly reflects the situation in the country at that time.

It was the best time of my life, but from a professional point of view the timing was unfortunate as UK was undertaking a worldwide re-assessment of the role of Defence Attachés, and indeed wider Embassy staff just at the time that I was in my post in Albania. This was of course outside my control, no matter how strongly I, and the Embassy hierarchy, defended the importance of being "resident" rather than occasionally visiting from a "hub" somewhere outside the country. Inevitably, this disappointing situation greatly hampered what resources might be available for me to bid for, but many other British Attachés in other countries during those three years faced the same. I am sure that the lack of material support I could offer must have reflected on how some of my Albanian interlocutors considered my effectiveness, especially as resources had not previously been so tight, and indeed from what I have heard the situation improved a couple of years later. Did the hard work I put in contribute to the improvement sometime after – bearing in mind time-lags for budgets and policy changes – I have no idea. In this timing, I was therefore extremely unfortunate as no one wanted to be more of a friend to Albania than me! I felt like I was working with one hand tied behind my back. Nevertheless, I hope that the places for Albanian students on hard-to-get courses in UK were useful, the visit of a British warship memorable, the visit of a British military unit for joint training worthwhile, the positive and optimistic reports I sent back to UK every month resulted in a different mindset and perhaps had a positive influence in the longer term, and my straight-forward and honest approach a good example.

I think it probably took many of my Albanian interlocutors quite some time to fully believe that I played everything "with a straight bat", as we would say in England. I was always honest. I wasn't throwing spin balls. I wasn't playing games. If I would say I would try to help, I did, to the best of my ability and given the circumstances which might be out of my control. If I offered advice, it was genuine. If I spoke in-confidence, that is exactly what I did. And if something was told to me in-confidence it has remained exactly that, even to this day. I cannot recall the exact quotation but there is something about "everyone who smiles at you wants something in return" and some have this so in-grained in their psyche that they cannot believe that someone might be wanting nothing in return, just honesty and friendship! Indeed, many of the other "players" fitted this quotation exactly! I absolutely refused to play games telling one person one thing and something completely different to someone else in order to cause division or gain some concocted advantage or false "friendship". When I bid to London for funds I stated my case honestly and accurately as to why they were needed. I know for a fact that this had not always been the case, and after my requests were repeatedly refused I could understand why others had perhaps seen fit to bend the truth, but I refused to lie to London, just as I would not lie to Albania.

I became close friends with one important and well-known Albanian, often visiting him unofficially, and thoroughly enjoying each other's company, simply because, as he once told me, so many others, of all nationalities, only visited him for some hidden reason, but he knew that I was trustworthy and honest....and I was. He shared some thoughts and ideas with me in-confidence and which I will never repeat, such is my respect for him and the principle of confidentiality. Controversial though he was in many people's eyes, I witnessed first-hand how modestly he lived, and how genuinely he wanted to work for the benefit of the country and Albanian people.

Perhaps some would accuse me of being overly naïve or holding outdated ideas of honour, respect, honesty, selfless service, and integrity. So be it – I am who I am. If any of those in the Albanian Ministry of Defence, politicians, or other agencies who knew me read this, I hope with hindsight that they now see that I was always a *true* friend and my words were *always* honest, and that my motivation was *never* for self-aggrandizement or popularity. Also, my "besa" was in accordance with the best traditions of Albanian custom. If I promised something, I abided by it, whether that was in regards to confidentiality, privacy, "off the record" talks, or whatever. Even so many years later my promise has remained intact.

So no, my decision to avoid any work-related stories, of which there are many, is not based on concerns for any secrecy of my own work, I have *nothing* to hide in that regard, but out of respect for some of the wonderful personalities I was privileged to work with, Albanian and foreigners. Some are still involved in their professions. Rightly or wrongly, in writing this slim volume I am concerned that if I mention one name, then some might wrongly theorize why I might not mention another? Or what might seem to me to be an innocent and humorous anecdote might be twisted and taken out of context. I would love to mention a string of names, some of whom have remained in contact to this day, but have decided not to, at least not in this volume. You know who you are my friends, and I count those who have remained in contact with me as dear friends.

I have avoided any attempt to sensationalize. I leave that for others, and more about this below.

I have recently enjoyed reading a book about Albania post-communism and the author is clearly extremely well connected and an expert in his field. I don't dispute this at all, but if I recounted some of the accounts from my own personal experience, my contacts and sources, my version of the same story might differ widely from his, in some particulars. Perhaps the story I have included in this book about "The British in Albania During World War Two" touches on this – I had the most lively discussions with Albanians on this subject, and their views were all valid. Equally, I had discussions on this same subject with British and other nationalities who failed to consider the situation from an Albanian perspective and consequently formed completely different conclusions. The bottom-line being that two people's perspectives of the same event(s) may greatly affect how it is perceived.

I very briefly mention another book which was one of the most readily available books about modern Albania and which was consequently one of the first books I read about the country I came to love. I refuse to note its title or give it shelf space. I discussed it with three of my most respected Albanian friends in some detail, and whilst the view was that whilst some of the awful events he so gleefully and graphically described might indeed have actually happened to him, the book was cover to cover sensationalism, with no balance, and simply criticism of the whole nation and people, and this is clearly inaccurate. Indeed, my trusted friends were justifiably angry about this book and disappointed that it was one of the first books I had read about the Albanian people. Yes, some dreadful things have happened, even in Albania's recent history, including some events which I personally witnessed, but to trash a whole nation because of those tragic dark events is unfair and unrealistic. However, I am sure the author has earned a decent sum from writing such sensationalism. Is it not accurate to suggest, dear reader, that any of us could pick any country in the world and find a specific event or time period or group of people which was, or are, abhorrent, desperate, shocking, cruel, embarrassing, and every other negative expression we can think of, and if we wrote solely about such things, especially if it was from a country which most people know little about, and we don't put any context, background, or explanation as to "how" or "why", the result would be a completely unfair and damaging account, even if factually it was undeniable.

Dare I say this – in my three years in the country I saw a number of foreigners who behaved with arrogance and aired an attitude of superiority which quite frankly made me feel ashamed to associate with them. Some talked up their own self-importance to impress and gain advantage. Many had the most superficial knowledge of the country, its people, history and culture and yet expressed their inaccurate, misleading or biased views with the attitude and impression of expertise. I am somewhat reminded of a line in Edith Durham's book, "Twenty Years of Balkan Tangle" (first published in 1920), in which she mentions Count Bollati, then Italian Minister to Montenegro. She wrote,

> "He loathed Cetinje and explained that he had accepted [the post] *"only as one better than Buenos Aires because nearer to Rome."*

She then quotes him,

> *"Your method of seeing lands is undoubtedly the best* [traveling around the country], *but I am satisfied with what I see from the windows of the best hotel."*

She continues,

> *"Nor, unfortunately, was Count Bollati in any way unique in his tastes, a fact which may have affected the politics of Europe."*

Disappointingly, I witnessed that this same attitude continues, at least during my time in Albania. Delete "Cetinje" and insert "Tirana" and add the name of one of the most well-known hotels there, and the picture hasn't changed! Add to that the disappointing but commonplace attitude of a notable percentage that their own career progression is always going to be paramount and is therefore the key driver in their current work, regardless of location or position. Consequently, even though some worked long hours, and I am sure in their opinion were working with dedication, if one's main goal is to further one's own career it will undoubtedly colour what one does, how one does it, and what one reports back to those who can influence one's next appointment. The truth is not always what one's boss wants to hear, indeed in these current times it seems the truth is not what a large percentage of people want to hear – they want to hear whatever will reinforce their pre-conceived notions. And to report back sensationalised stories of dangerous escapades in which we can become the hero is much more likely to attract the attention of our personnel managers than a routine account of normalcy!

With sincere regret I once had to take steps against one charming fellow who dressed impeccably and was as polite as could be, but my sources gave me clear evidence that in the bars of Tirana in the evening he was telling stories about the work in the Embassy, including sections for which he had absolutely no responsibility, and even sometimes pretending to be in my position! This came to me from numerous sources, international and Albanian, on multiple occasions, and this was clearly completely unacceptable. I mention it because whilst one might think that this was a one-off case, sadly I suspect that to tell stories, true or untrue, to exaggerate and create legends around ourselves is a danger that is too much of a temptation for some in order to impress young women, gain kudos from other men, enhance careers, or to sell books! This intelligent young man was always accompanied by at least two others who also held diplomatic status, and this suggests that my theory that this was not a one-off case has credence. I regret having felt the need to take action, but multiple warnings were given with no effect, and his actions were unacceptable and diplomatically dangerous.

Nevertheless, clearly there is a balance to be found. One would be foolish to completely ignore all the warnings when visiting *any* country, be that of pickpockets in London, or advice for females not to walk alone in a dark park, or to be respectful and act with care in the mountains of Albania. I recall visiting Washington DC and once my few days work were finished I was joined by an Asian female friend for a couple of days leave. When I told my American colleagues they advised me in all seriousness which areas would be dangerous for me to be seen with an Asian woman as some would not like to see a mixed-race couple walking together even there in the centre of Washington DC, literally it was "turn left here and you are perfectly safe, but please do not turn right". I thought they were pulling my leg, but they were deadly serious – and look at the number of hate crimes against Asians in the last few years in the USA. I was disgusted in UK when I heard a story of mindless idiots injuring dogs and horses for no reason but for their own "entertainment". Here in Taiwan, my wife constantly tells me not to sound the car horn even when some lunatic in a flashy car does the most dangerous manoeuver threatening others' lives right in front of me. Why? Because it is not unknown for so-called "gangsters" to take offence and leap out of their car with baseball bats or worse, just because someone has dared to sound their horn at their dangerous driving. Just today a terrible local news story here recounted a tragic story of an adolescent who killed his grandmother after he asked her for some money and she, for the first time, refused him. I had my house in UK broken into twice, and a military quarter I inhabited in Germany burgled whilst I slept upstairs. In Amsterdam I had my car window broken right outside the hotel, and as I cleaned up the mess a local man told me they all leave their cars unlocked because, more often than not, drug addicts will break into cars just for somewhere to sleep! When I was working in Lithuania for a couple of months a Lithuanian soldier quickly grabbed my arm and told me to immediately leave a bar where I was quietly having a drink with my Sergeant one evening because some local men had decided to beat us up, just for being foreigners! In Nepal I had a death-threat made against me and hand delivered to my own guardroom! Also in Nepal, my predecessor was kidnapped by Maoist guerrillas. Once here in Taiwan some thugs arrived in our area with a police vehicle escorting them and when a few of us stood in front of them in an attempt to prevent them from destroying a park area where their "employer" wished to illegally build, they threatened us. The other locals backed off, I didn't, and one of the idiots pulled a knife and lunged at me, right in front of the policeman. When I still didn't back down, the thugs were allowed to quietly leave, whilst I was taken to the police station to make a statement! "Would you recognise the man?", "Yes, but so would you – you arrived with him!" And I have no confidence that the translated statement I was forced to sign was a true record of what I had said – the local resident who was with me was prevented from checking it for me. A couple of years ago a very large international religious organisation in India wanted me to take on an on-going internal investigation of corruption and malpractice, resident in India for 6 months a year. I met all the top leaders of the organisation, and most were very encouraging, but when I met the local management committee (which comprised of Indians and internationals) and told them I could only succeed with their full support, I was met by, at best, silence. I had already identified at least two members of the committee as being as corrupt as can be! A day or two after the meeting a friend who was resident there advised me that these local "gangsters", who were part of the management, were already asking questions about where I was staying and what my routine was. He advised me to leave as soon as possible. The previous (American) chap who had attempted to take this task on had fled the country in fear for his life, and the charming, modest (Indian) gentleman who was nominally holding the job until I arrived had been beaten up several times and hospitalised once. In early 2021 we saw the storming of the Capital in the USA – imagine the internationals' reports back to their capital cities had that occurred in Albania! 14,861 gun-related homicides occurred in the US in 2019. Need I go on? My point is, it is so easy to highlight all the terrible goings-on, in any country, and all too often forgetting that the situation in one's own country is little better, if any!

The impressive mountains of northern Albania.

It must be said however, I personally witnessed some visitors in Albania who were carelessly blasé in their attitude, believing themselves to be somehow impervious to the potential dangers of local heart-felt and deeply held traditions. Not long before I arrived there was one chap with diplomatic status who had to be removed from the country without delay after he upset a young lady's brother by his somewhat carefree attitude towards her. Such things can lead to a rather personal and rapid lesson in the traditions of the Kanun! Let's just say that removing him from the country almost certainly saved his life, literally.

Some believed that they were somehow *protected* because they were American, British, German or whatever. If one assumes an air of arrogant superiority, especially at a time of tension and internal confusion and frustration, unable to speak the language and ignorant or disregarding of deeply held customs and what is considered acceptable behaviour, is it any wonder that some have strayed into trouble?

Others truly believed they had sufficient knowledge to avoid mishap in this ancient land because they had scanned over a guidebook for an hour and had exchanged a few emails with an Albanian! One person who had spent a grand total of five days in the country once spoke to me as if they were an expert in Albanian affairs and spewed forth all the most exaggerated and fictitious dribble imaginable. Sadly, I was told that the Albanian "friend" this lady had been in contact with had also exaggerated all sorts of nonsense, even claiming he had been jailed because of his recent writing and consequently sought political asylum abroad (and succeeded) for fear of persecution. I checked him out and he had never been in jail in his life! But this had been told to this mutual friend, who now repeats to all who will listen about the persecution of writers today, and how dangerous it was for anyone of faith to live there. Even when I objected she still chose to believe this other story. I guess the writer was an author of fiction and lost contact with reality and didn't care one iota what a negative image of his own country he gave to gullible foreigners. I suppose, like the young man in the bars of Tirana, he thought it made his own life more interesting, and some will believe it because they want to believe it – back to the theory of the "post-truth era" in which we live. Incredible!

This is a complex country, an ancient people, with a complicated history, be in no doubt about that. Not everything is good, and not everything is bad. What is good is exceptionally so, but what is bad can be shocking for those seeing the country through rose-tinted spectacles.

I will briefly mention one memory here which hurt me at the time but is perhaps worth telling. Once I was discussing some facet of the country with one of the very intelligent and well-educated Albanian members of the Embassy staff. I remember her cold response so clearly,

> *"But you will never really understand what it means to be Albanian. You will never really understand why so many of my generation just want to leave the country, no matter what. You cannot understand, because after three years you will leave."*

I don't wish to sound overly melodramatic dear reader, but it was as if she had stabbed me in the heart. By the time of this exchange I had traveled all over the country several times and was in love with the country. I had visited places she had hardly heard of, places where no foreigners had been for decades, areas which were still at that time considered too remote or dangerous for a foreigner to travel. I had studied the traditions deeply, especially those of the northern mountains where they still played an important role - I knew all this probably better than her. I spoke the language reasonably well, and if I didn't say too much (!) could pass myself off as an Albanian. I identified myself with this country, her country. I asked my friend when she had last visited Shkodra or Bajram Çurri, or the mountains of the north – she had never done so in her life, and had no desire to do so. I asked what she knew about the law of the Kanun, or mountain traditions – the very thought disgusted her. I enquired about how much she had studied the complexities of the various Albanian groups which fought in World War Two, and the part which foreigners played. Her response was simply that the British were responsible for the decades of communism which her people had been forced to endure after the war – but the reality is much more complex than that as I hope to explain in the chapter on this subject. As her cultural background was "Tosk" (from the south) I asked how much she had studied "Gheg" culture (from the north) – she thought it irrelevant to her life in the capital city, Tirana. She acknowledged all I said and agreed that I had a greater knowledge than most, and that I had seen more of the country than the majority of Albanians ever would. Actually, I could feel that my Embassy friend did indeed have things inside her which I could certainly never understand and which she would probably never try to explain to me. Afterall, I was just a work colleague, although I hope she considered me a true friend as well. Somehow I could feel her suffering and her great disappointments in life – I could see it in her eyes when she talked, when others might just have seen a pretty face and fashionable clothes. But I also saw in her eyes that some of the disappointment was perhaps with some foreigners whose behaviour she had hoped would be more honest and honourable, only to discover that they were no better than those from whom she was trying to escape. I was aware of whispered comments and heard of parties at which some foreigners made presumptions based on how this young lady (fashionably) dressed, and it sickened and disgusted me. I never attended such parties, not once, but I heard the snickering and disrespectful comments about this person whom I respected and liked, and on more than one occasion I took fellow Englishmen to task for being so ignorant. Anyhow, after my heartfelt defence, she simply lowered her eyes and quietly repeated,

> *"No matter how much you study, how much you read, how much you travel around Albania, you will never really understand."*

This short tale has no conclusion except to say, I try.

How much does a wealthy young man or woman who has grown up in post-communist Tirana, perhaps living a privileged life gained through their parents money (however that was gained), driving around in their flashy car and with an apartment or villa in the most prestigious area of the capital city, truly understand about the struggles of a farmer in some remote area, or the family still embroiled in a blood feud in the mountains of the north, or the young man whose family have lived for a thousand years in a certain area and who wishes to do nothing but remain there for as long as he can provide for his family? Sadly, I suspect many probably don't even care.

I mentioned above that I spoke the language reasonably well – oh how I wish I still did – so let me share one amusing aside. Once my wife and I were invited to an intimate birthday party for a VVIP – there were maybe 20 Albanians present, plus us as the only foreigners. When the meal finished, after about two hours, one of the Albanian female guests asked my wife in all seriousness, "But why did you marry an Albanian?" Oh how I laughed! I guess I hadn't said too much!

As I started to compile this volume and decided what to include, a few questions arose, and I will attempt to answer them here in case they crop up in your own mind as you read this.

One question an Albanian friend asked me very forcefully was why I rarely wrote about anything negative, and on the occasions that I did comment on such issues he accused me (with some justification) of not dwelling on it. Giving me what he saw as constructive criticism he said that he felt it made my writing too superficial, like a tourist who only saw the good things, and he knew very well that my knowledge of the country was much deeper than that. He expected me to expose and explore the negativities in the depth he knew I understood. I respect his viewpoint and do understand that it is an all too common mistake for "an outsider" to see a superficial aspect of a society and mistake it for a deeper understanding, but I sincerely hope that over the years I spent in Albania, and the seriousness with which I studied and indeed immersed myself in the culture and traditions, I *did* understood something deeper. Yet, the comment from this friend was fair, to an extent. My answer is that I deliberately choose to write about the positives not because I am blind to the rest, but because so much is already written about the negatives that, and it greatly saddens to me to write this, it unfairly adversely colours the impression of this country and its people which I came to love.

In fact, I am not at all blind to the problems, challenges, faults and suffering. Yet, in all my travels around the country, including to some of the most troubled and remote areas, in three years I never received anything but courtesy and impeccable hospitality. Yes, I had made the effort to learn to speak the language reasonably well – enough that I could travel and talk to local people over a coffee in a relaxed fashion without interpreters or any signs of "officialdom". I had also studied the culture and traditions, and perhaps my sincerity and genuine love for the place shone through – I don't know, but I hope it did. I had more Albanian friends than English and of course we talked about many of the problems. I know full well how real they were, and sadly many still are. Of course, because of the nature of my work I was very familiar with the machinations and intrigues of internal Albanian politics. I am reasonably well read with regards to Albanian history and know that so much of it had been written in blood. I have some knowledge of the complexities of the betrayals and dishonesty of the Great Powers and other neighbouring countries in their dealings with Albania, especially in the first 20 years or so of the 20th century – and I suspect some of those attitudes still prevail, albeit more hidden.

I know clearly about the tragedies of blood feuds, and how in more recent years the Kanun has all too often been used as an excuse, deliberately or otherwise, for what is not "honour" but simply common criminality and even murder. But blood feuds have been written about all too often by foreigners with nothing more than the flimsiest understanding and all too frequently simply sensationalized superficiality.   Please do not misunderstand me, I know this is a genuine and tragic issue even today, but it shouldn't define "Albania". If one actually reads the Kanun - and I suspect most foreigners who write about it have not - there is only one section which deals with gjakmarrja (blood feuds), whilst the vast majority of the content discusses land ownership issues, access to water, respecting guests in one's home, and so on. I am not glorifying the Kanun, simply attempting to put some perspective on it, and yes, there are other parts of the Kanun, such as the way it talks about women, which are of course totally unacceptable today. But it also protects women, and yet today some even involve women and girls in "gjakmarrja", whereas in fact the Kanun is absolutely clear on this issue – females cannot kill or be killed in blood feuds.

I heard first hand of some of the incredibly terrible experiences some had been through, and not forgetting that communism had only ended 15 years before I arrived, so for most people this was still well within their recent memory.

I was in Shkodra during one of the elections and through my contacts there I was whisked off with them to any reports of "problems", and so saw the best and worst of that at first hand. The best were those who were determined to see fair elections no matter what the provocations might be. The worst were the corrupt bullies who would stop at nothing to gain power and influence. I could dwell on the latter and add to the all too frequent negative press, or I could see the bravery and determination of the former and show them my respect by writing about some of the great things about Albania. I choose the latter path. And forgive me but I have to say, the images of former-President Trump's supporters attacking Capitol Hill in January 2021, leaving five dead and 138 injured, and with four police officers who responded to the riot committing suicide within seven months, was far worse than anything I ever saw in Albania. Also the on-going refusal amongst some to accept the results of the 2020 US Presidential election.   I am not commenting on US politics – but are these recent examples witnessed across the world any better than the democracy and democratic processes, and yes – problems, in Albania?

I was the first foreigner to arrive at the site of the Gërdec ammunition site tragedy, and that dreadful incident still leaves many question marks in my mind but I am advised not to talk more about this extremely sad event. My sincere and heartfelt condolences to the families who lost loved ones – infinitely more important than the nasty reality of politics and power-play.

I was on the receiving end of attempts to bribe, and personally saw far too much corruption, and some seemed to be left incredulous that I was never tempted and would never budge from what I knew to be right. But this was not just an "Albanian problem" as some would have you believe - I know that some foreigners *were* accepting bribes, which probably explains why some were so surprised that I was immune to such approaches. I saw some stoop to the temptation of corruption, or at least being less than honest, in order to "buy" friendship and influence. So were they any better than those they criticize so freely? Absolutely not.

My heart cries over the lack of infrastructure planning that I witnessed, and I can only wonder how "permission" for some of the buildings was ever gained, especially seeing such a gloriously beautiful coastline so blighted. I hope this situation has now improved. And yet in my opinion Albanians seem to have an in-built appreciation of beauty, even if they don't talk about it. In nearly every home I had the privilege to visit, whether wealthy or poor, I found them to be impeccably clean and decorated, much more so than in most other places I have lived. I have several friends who have been desperately trying to retain their homes and land against all the questionable officialdom, and yes I am aware of the arguments over ownership before and after the communist regime, etc., but I have also seen some cases where I strongly suspect other influences were playing their part. Yet whilst these honest friends and their families are suffering in their fight to retain what is clearly theirs, others are getting fat and rich, building ill-planned and ill-conceived structures which are damaging the beauty and reputation of the whole country.

But again, do not think this was solely an Albanian problem. I was very close to one well-known Albanian who was conned out of huge sums of assets and money in a property development project led by a British man.

I visited some of the poorest and desperate of communities.

Conversely, I was close friends with extremely talented and dedicated people, Albanians and foreigners, who worked tirelessly in their efforts to build a better society, increase trust, transparency, the rule of law, the rights of women and minority groups, and confidence in the judicial system, to improve medical, education and social infrastructures, and rid the country of its poisonous influences. Sadly, I also saw that all too often their efforts came to naught, resources wasted or syphoned off, with corruption lining the pockets of the selfish, at the expense of the wider society.

Not all is good, not all is bad, so don't judge a whole nation on the corrupt and criminal behavior of a small percentage, but don't be a naive foreigner either.

I have artist and writer friends who have told me countless stories of what life was like during the communist regime. I saw at first hand the thugs and the bullies. I have personally seen people in the highest positions in the country totally ignored the day after they were no longer in office.

I was involved in secret meetings, in quiet restaurants miles from anywhere and requests to me not to use my official car, not because we were discussing anything secret, but for fear of who might be watching whom and then trying to construe something from it. And even more coffees in small cafes rather than meeting in an office, often for similar reasons. Such was the paranoia at times.

I am aware of all this, and sadly much more, but I choose not to write about it because I also saw a very different Albania. I mention these things here as I do not want you, dear reader, to think I am blind to the negatives and naively only saw Albanian society with an unrealistic romanticism of fiction. But I will not dwell on them in this small book. I saw the beauty and pride of the people. I reveled in its history and traditions and the most glorious landscapes. I worked and became friends with some fantastic people, warm, generous, welcoming and scrupulously honest, and I treasure the friendships I made. I feel just as passionate about the country today as I did when I lived there. This is what I wish to share with you.

I recently read on an Albanian on-line forum a discussion about whether traditional Albanian culture was dead, and I was bitterly disappointed to read comment after comment that traditional values and customs were irrelevant and only dragging Albania backwards. Commentator after commentator said that the US, Italy, Germany, UK, or anywhere else in Europe was the future, and traditional Albania was a relic of the past and worthless and the only future worth living was to leave. I was so sad to read this. We *must* move forward, we *must* make progress for the benefit of our citizens, but I can only hope that these were youngsters merely expressing the folly of youth. I hope that with greater life experience they will realise the beauty and uniqueness of traditional Albanian values and customs and find a way to weave those traditions into a modern society in which they will feel happy and proud. Discard those things and what is left? What would there be to make Albania unique?

Yet, despite all the negative things I have personally seen, I became fascinated by Albania and its people, more than "fascinated" – I felt I belonged there. I have never experienced such perfect hospitality anywhere in the world. I came to love the varying landscapes, and quickly grew to respect the harsh and rugged mountains of the north as well as the gentler hills and vales of the south. I developed close friendships and retain some to this day. I met some amazing people who, despite all the obstacles, remained determined to forge a better society. I was welcomed into the homes of many. I was never made to feel that my religious beliefs as a Buddhist, nor my resultant dietary restrictions, were an obstacle or something to be mocked. Although so often frustrated in my attempts to learn the language perfectly, I came to greatly admire and love it – I only wish I could speak it better today! I loved the beautiful coastline from north to south, and was entranced by the history of so many incredible sites from Butrint in the south to Rozafa Castle in the north, from Gjirokaster to Petrele and Kruja. I loved the lakes which are plenty and of incredible beauty, and the virgin forests and ice cold rivers as they flowed down from the mountains. I developed a love for the passion of the music and have tried to teach myself how to play the çifteli, and I was in awe of the talent of so many artists, musicians and writers. I met some wonderful people who were honest and determined, dedicated and loyal, visionary and inspiring. I can only hope and pray that they will rise to the top.

So for all the faults and problems, I love Albania and I hope this impression shines through when you read this small book.

May the Albanian double-headed eagle always fly with pride and strength.

FIRST ENCOUNTERS WITH ALBANIA

It was a warm day in early summer, the morning after I first stepped foot in the country, and I was being driven in a British Embassy vehicle to Shkodra where I was to spend the next month living with a family I had never met before. The intention of this part of my training was "language immersion", in other words to immerse myself into the Albanian culture and language and hopefully therefore make progress with my language studies before I was to officially move to the capital city, Tirana, a few months later. But having been told that the family with whom I would stay didn't speak a word of English I wasn't sure if it would be "immersion" or "submersion"!

Strangely, the homestay was organised for me not by the British Embassy but by Antoine Rozès who headed the Organisation for Security and Cooperation in Europe (OSCE) field station in the northern city of Shkodra. He also organised an Albanian language teacher for me, who would teach me for an hour or two each day. Antoine and I were to become good friends, and remain so to this day.

As I looked out of the car windows I was struck by the rugged and imposing beauty of the mountains appearing in the distance. The highway was better than I had expected, and the landscape definitely so. I had only arrived in Albania the evening before flying from London to Vienna, and changing aircraft to Tirana. My other colleagues with whom I had been undertaking some of the non-country specific training, and who were selected as Defence and Military Attaches in other countries around the world had enjoyed several relaxing days with the chap they were going to take over from, often unofficially meeting key interlocutors so that they could hit the ground running on their official arrival a few months later. This was not the case for me and I was being introduced to no one and, for whatever reason, the intention was to get me out of Tirana and up to Shkodra as quickly as possible. As things would pan out, I have no regrets about this whatsoever, but at the time it seemed highly unusual and I was somewhat surprised. It was the proverbial "being thrown in at the deep end".

As the landscape flashed by and my mind wandered I couldn't help but recall some of the negative and scare-mongering stories I had been told. Such stories make an imprint on one's mind before one can develop one's own views, impressions and experiences. Has it not always been the case that some deliberately talk up the horrors and dangers in order to make their own lives seem more interesting, at least in some cases, whilst others never develop their own deeper understanding one way nor the other. I was sitting in the back seat when, after about an hour into the journey, the cell-phone in the front of the vehicle rang. After the conversation the one who had taken the call turned to me and said, "The police officer with whom you were scheduled to meet for lunch today was killed in a car bomb a couple of hours ago. We'll drop you off direct at your homestay."

I had read a book a couple of months before, the name of which I refuse to mention – some readers will know to which book I am referring – written by an American, and one of the most exaggerated and one-sided books about Albania that one could possibly imagine (I mentioned it in the lengthy Introduction). My wonderful Albanian teachers in London were quite angry at the very mention of "that book" and indeed, despite the fact that I later gathered quite a collection of Albania related books, I absolutely refuse to give that awful piece of sensationalism shelf space. Actually, now I feel quite sorry for the author that he appears never to have experienced the great things about the country and its people and history which I was to come to enjoy so much in the next three years. Yet here we were, heading to this "infamous" city, the police contact I was supposed to meet had just been killed, and all the stories I had heard were buzzing in my head. Was "that book" actually not quite as fictional in its descriptions as I had been led to believe? Time would tell.

But still the wonderful landscape seemed to be making an inexplicable connection to my heart, even from the backseat of a speeding 4 x 4. We passed the turn for Kruja some time back – little did I know then about the history of that magical place, and now that I live the other side of the world, how I wish I could visit there again. Oh, how easy it is to take things for granted when they are on your doorstep. Kruja, home to the Illyrian tribe of the Albani in ancient times, and later a place of history and legend of the national hero Skanderbeg, of wars and conquests and re-captures. Truly an amazing place and I will return to it later in this book.

Now a glimpse of a single small road sign to Ishull i Lezhes caught my eye for some reason, not knowing then that "Diella's" restaurant there would become one of my favourite places in the whole of Albania, indeed with no word of over-exaggeration one of my favourite places in Europe. I was amazed a few weeks ago, sitting here in Taiwan, when she appeared on one of the cable TV stations, being visited by one of the British celebratory chefs! Skip forward a year or two and a few of my international colleagues asked me to take them out somewhere for lunch. I guess I had developed a bit of a reputation for having got to know the country better than most. I decided to take them to my favourite place - "Diella's". I had been there a dozen times or more by then, and I was completely flabbergasted when my friends were reduced to near apoplexy when I turned off the main Tirana-Lezhe road onto the small and dusty track which led to this little paradise. Did they really believe that something dreadful lay around the next corner – how very sad! Maybe they had read "that book" or been persuaded by other negative propaganda.

Anyhow, back to this, my first of many road trips in the country I came to love. A sharp right bend and there at the top of the hill in front of us, just before the main road curved left again, were the remains of the castle of Lezhë – a treasure fallen into a poor state of dis-repair, but a treasure none the less. I remember from my tourist guidebook that the history of Lezhë stretched back around 2,400 years, and it was the resting place of the great hero, Skanderbeg.

On the journey went. Finally sight of the Drin and Buna rivers, and then over to my left I got my first glimpse of the wonderful Shkodra Lake which appeared to stretch out forever. An ever so pretty and colourful church appeared, the Church of Our Lady of Good Counsel, sheltered under the hill to our right, on top of which loomed Rozafa Castle. I will write about both in this book. Then a brief flash of a Roma community to the left – a community I would later visit several times, and finally into the city which would be my home for the next month.

View south from Rozafa Castle.

The stories of the ominous nature of this city, which I would feel privileged to call my home, were such that many diplomats would not even visit, at least not then. "Out of bounds", I was told! Such an un-envious reputation flooded my mind once more as we passed some typical communist era apartment blocks, looking oppressive and grey.

Then appeared what was obviously a fairly newly constructed mosque, its silver dome shining brightly in the sun and making such a contrast from the grey blocks and all other architecture in the city as to appear almost incongruous to the scene, as if it didn't belong there. This was the Ebu Bekër Mosque and had been constructed ten years earlier, 1994-1995[1]. It had been built on the site of the Mosque of Fushë Çela which had been destroyed during the Communist regime, and which had not only been the largest mosque in the city but also one of great significance, attracting many Moslem scholars from all over the region. I was to discover that the new mosque can accommodate up to 1300 people, and its two minarets are approximately 41 meters in height, with its dome an impressive 24 meters in height. Impossible to miss!

Then we were into the high street. The hotel where I was supposed to meet the now tragically and so recently deceased police officer was pointed out to me. My first impression was of surprise at some of the beautiful architecture, the details of the decoration on the buildings, and the pastel colours, and I was reminded of some old Italian towns. The impression was slightly marred as the block-paved sidewalks were a mess (they were later replaced, but after my three years) and a few buildings were boarded up, including the old bank, and with ominous signs of serious smoke damage in some. I was to enjoy leisurely strolling along this street in the early evening "gjiro" when it seemed that half the city appeared, dressed in their finest clothes. Sometimes I would be accompanied by one of my homestay ladies, who I would come to think of as my "Albanian aunties".

The vehicle pulled over and we were joined by Antoine. This fine French gentleman, who remains one of my closest friends to

---

[1] The Ebu Bekër Mosque was renovated in 2008.

this very day, had arranged everything perfectly. One amusing story occurred in the few weeks leading up to this home-stay. I will be diplomatic and simply say that all my attaché colleagues going to other countries had received finely programmed itineraries weeks earlier, and it was becoming something of a joke whenever I met my colleagues on the various courses and briefings, "So, do you know what you are doing yet?" I didn't! As the time for me to fly to Albania was literally within two weeks, and I had heard nothing, one might imagine that my patience was wearing slightly thin. About the only piece of information I was given was that I would be collected from the airport and would spend the first night in Tirana, and I was given Antoine's contact details and told he was arranging everything, even though he was employed by OSCE, not Her Majesty! Never mind – I just wanted to know what was happening. So I contacted him and the conversation went something like this:

"Hi, thanks so much for helping. I really appreciate it."

"My pleasure. Looking forward to meeting you."

"Likewise. So, about my homestay, has it been arranged? I fly in under two weeks time and so far I have been told absolutely nothing."

"Yes"

"Err, ok, can you tell me anything about where I will be staying please?"

"With two unmarried sisters."

"Err, really?" (trying not to sound nervously surprised!)

"Yes. I have to go now, but let's chat again in a couple of days. I just need to firm up some details."

Gosh, two unmarried sisters! Not at all what I was expecting to hear. I needed to know more. So in the next conversation, and trying to sound nonchalant:

> *"So, thanks again, but two unmarried sisters ... err....is that ok? I thought Albanian culture would be sensitive about a man staying in the same house with an unmarried woman, let alone two of them."*

A mischievous laugh at the other end of the phone, clearly relishing my discomfort.

> *"It will be fine, don't worry."*

> *"Sure?"*

> *"Yes"*

> *"Absolutely sure?"*

> *"Yes"*

and after a perfectly timed pause he added,

> *"both are considerably older than you, an old Shkodran family, and are charming and very respectable and honourable ladies."*

Perhaps cowardly I couldn't help but sighing a great sigh of relief. I didn't want "complications" before I had even begun! I was quickly to think of them as my own family and do so until this day.

Anyhow, I digress.

Back into the 4 x 4 again and 5 minutes later we pulled up outside a high walled compound. The doorbell was rung and I admit to feeling just a tad nervous as I waited to meet my "adopted family" for the first time. Two impeccably dressed, smiling ladies, greeted me warmly and we were led inside. Their courtyard was spotlessly swept and there was a profusion of flowers in various pots. The bungalow was well painted in a sunny ochre colour, and as we entered I could see the pride with which they kept their home. I was shown to my room which was very spacious, well furnished, and with some nice paintings on the wall. They offered us all refreshments, but my "host" from Tirana seemed anxious to get back on the road as soon as he could. My cases were brought to my room and with a "See you in a month" he left, literally within 2 or 3 minutes! My only other contact with Tirana in the whole month was a week or ten days later when I discovered that no arrangement had been made to pay for my accommodation or language tuition (from official funds of course) which was causing me some considerable embarrassment. After more excuses and being told how busy they all were, I had no option but to almost demand that the agreed money be brought to me immediately, or "Put me through to the Ambassador, I am sure he can arrange it if you can't." That did the trick and the money was delivered within 24 hours.

I very quickly discovered that I couldn't have been with a more hospitable family. Over the next month I really did think of them as my family, and even now, so many years later, I regret so much that we have lost contact – I am sure that I regret it more than they realise. I have sent them Christmas cards and a letter every year, but this last year I met someone who knew them and was told that they have never received a single one. That saddens me.

Over the course of the month I came to love Lake Shkodra, the largest lake in the Balkans, fantastic restaurants along its banks and with such beautiful and unrivalled views. Even though I am a vegetarian I was never ever made to feel that I was troublesome, and it was almost dreamlike to while away the hours sitting there, with perfect hospitality and waters so calm stretching beyond forever. Honestly, I could have happily made a home right there and never left - glorious! I came to understand something of the rich culture, music, poetry, art and humour of Shkodra. It may sound ridiculous, but whenever I saw Rozafa Castle (either during that month or throughout the three years that I lived in Tirana) it felt like I was "home" - Shkodra. Indeed, after I had assumed my post for some time, some wags in the Embassy started calling me "Marku Shkodrani"!

The author with his Albanian "family".

I made visits to the 18th century 100 metre long bridge, "Ura e Mesit", and was fascinated by its asymmetrical pattern of 13 arches. I allowed my imagination to run riot with thoughts of the centuries of people who had passed over it before me. I will write about this in a later chapter.

I made my first of several visits to the little village of Vermosh with Antoine and some of his friends, over the mountains north of Shkodra, and close to the border with Montenegro. I witnessed a landscape that was so breathtakingly beautiful, and the mountain road with switchback after switchback so fantastically rugged that it seemed to lead me into another world. We swam in a cool mountain pool at the foot of a waterfall which was simply idyllic. We stayed with a family in the village and witnessed yet again the very best of the Albanian tradition of hospitality which I hope is never lost.

The dam at Vau i Dejes showed signs of more difficult times in its recent history, but instead of seeing the negative, I focused on the positive, and to see the reservoir stretching out, around hills and mountains the likes of which I had never seen before moved me greatly. Watching the children walking on the narrow hillside tracks made me ponder on how hard life must be, and how easy and dangerous it is for a visitor to see the romanticism of the harsh landscape without acknowledging the reality and starkness of life. I questioned myself whether I could live there, and I could understand why so many had left, but still I couldn't help hoping and praying that small communities would remain for many generations to come, keeping traditional lifestyles alive. When I moved to Nepal after my three years in Albania I saw many communities in the Himalayan foothills disappearing as the younger generation moved to the capital city, leaving no one to look after the older family members and causing societal question marks about whose role it should be to provide for those old and infirm. I witnessed in Nepal how it takes imagination and determination for the middle generation to return and find ways to generate income and livelihoods, often through innovative schemes to attract tourists. In that Himalayan country there were thankfully some who had worked abroad (often as Gurkhas in the British army, with whom I served) who were proud and felt strongly about their "roots" and created fund raising schemes. They poured in time, money and energy to rebuild small sustainable villages which would otherwise simply disappear. Yes, often this resulted in changes and some bemoaned the blight on the traditional Himalayan landscape which the road building schemes brought to areas previously unreachable except on foot. But at least the communities were being kept alive, whereas others simply perished. Apologies for this aside, but another interesting thing often seen in those communities in Nepal were "Ama Toli" (literally, "mother's parties"). These were the women of the village who as soon as they became aware of tourists staying their village would visit and ask if the trekkers would welcome their "Ama Toli" in the evening. Usually the answer was "yes", in which case the women would return at sunset and sing and sometimes dance to traditional folk songs. In exchange the tourists would offer them a monetary gift and oftentimes food. Interestingly, even though singing and dancing is more traditionally a male activity in that region, the women organised this rather than the men because they feared the men would immediately spend the money on alcohol, whereas these organised "Ama Toli" would save the money to benefit the whole community!

Anyhow, back to Albania. One day I was delighted to be enthusiastically greeted by whom I presume was the caretaker of the *Leaden Mosque*, also called the Buşatli Mehmet Pasha Mosque. Built between 1773 - 1774 and restored at least three times since then, this treasure has suffered over its life, but at least had not been totally destroyed during the communist regime. The ground on which it is built is only a couple of metres above sea-level and prone to flooding, and indeed it was almost surrounded by water the first time I saw it, making it seem somewhat forlorn, but on subsequent visits, of which there were several, it was dry and looked considerably better. In fact, this was the area of the original town, although almost no signs of it remain. Archaeological excavations have revealed part of the ancient city wall and signs of the old houses and buildings, but only this proud old mosque remains. This is the largest ancient mosque in Albania and the only example with a courtyard enclosed within the main structure – a sign of a prestigious mosque. The inscription above the door to the prayer hall records the restoration and repair in 1863 and was not the original stone. Originally the domes would have been covered in lead, but this has been removed at some time and is now concrete. Sadly, the minaret was demolished during communist days. It was wonderful to see that some people were determined to preserve and keep it alive.

Leaden Mosque, also called the Buşatli Mehmet Pasha Mosque, Shkodra.

Later I was privileged enough to be invited into one of those grey communist apartments to visit a family, and I was very pleasantly surprised at the interior. Nicely decorated with more pride than most houses I had visited anywhere, impeccably clean and tidy, and more comfortable than I could have imagined. I was also treated to the legendary Albanian hospitality, unrivalled in the world. Suddenly the grayness didn't seem so oppressive after all, at least once inside.

My month passed by all too quickly, but something had really connected deep inside me. Even though I had been somewhat thrown into this city with little support except for that of my newly found friend, Antoine, I felt that I belonged here. Maybe that was the idea and, if it was, they did it well! Yes, it is illogical and maybe sounds unrealistically dramatic, but I felt it deeply - I could have happily just stayed there!

I returned to UK for a couple of months to finish my training and to undertake the second of my language exams, but I couldn't wait for the date when I was to return to Albania. I was excited to explore other parts of the country, but somehow, for some reason, Shkodra always felt like home, and even now I feel that part of me has remained there.

One footnote to this story was that I had been studying the ancient Albanian language intensely for some time before visiting, and the infamously complicated grammar had been drummed into me by my teachers. Yet, I came to learn that those from Shkodra, such as my wonderful homestay ladies, had a slightly different set of grammar rules in certain tenses and declensions. Add to that the beautiful Shkodran accent, which inevitably as I had spoken almost nothing but Albanian for a month, apart from the hours spent with Antoine, I had adopted. To see the horror on my teachers' faces during my first language lesson back in London really was quite a picture. They had worked so hard to try to give me a pure "capital city" standard Albanian, and there I was speaking like an old Shkodrani! I may return to that subject later.

THE LANGUAGE EXAM

I must tell this brief story before I proceed to stories within Albania.

I have just mentioned in the previous chapter that after my month in Shkodra I returned to UK for final briefings and to tackle the second language examination. Please be in no doubt, I am not in any way a linguist, but I threw myself into learning Albanian to the best of my ability. This ancient European language is one of those few which is unconnected to any other. In other words, there is nothing on which to hang one's hat. It really is learning a completely new language, in every respect. Yes, some words have been adopted from Italian, Greek or Turkish, but the language itself is said to stretch right back to the Illyrians.

Thoughtfully it was arranged that I would have a mix of male and female teachers, with slightly different accents, and it was agreed that I could take my lessons in London, one-to-one. My three wonderful language teachers, Edlira Babamusta-Gay, Blerina Piho, and Endrit Shijaku, were always careful to ensure I knew the correct Albanian word and not only the "adopted" word. Blerina would sometimes slap my knuckles with a ruler if I used an "adopted" word, although she now denies that!

Anyhow, I really worked hard. I didn't go anywhere without my vocabulary cards – a way of learning vocabulary – English words on one side of the card and Albanian words on the other. If I was walking down the street I would be flicking through my vocab cards, or a few minutes at lunchtime, or last thing at night, first thing in the morning – actually, even though I say it myself, I really did work hard. I would try to think in Albanian, and if I got stuck or wanted to check something I would send a telephone message to one of the teachers to verify. They also put in far more "out of classroom" hours with me than they were contracted to do with the demands of this determined student!

But as I have said, I am not a natural linguist, it was all down to hard work. Nor am I good at exams! The level I was studying to involved two sets of exams, both accredited by the University of Westminster. The first was at a rudimentary level which didn't phase me much as I knew how hard I was working, and that was passed easily.

The second was a few weeks after my return from the month in Shkodra and much more challenging as it was at a considerably higher level, and I knew that I had a tendency to get nervous in exams, no matter how well I knew the subject. Some other colleagues going to other countries and learning other languages were much more relaxed about the whole thing and one pointed out to me, "so if we fail our language exams, what are they going to do, select someone else and start the whole year's training again? I don't think so! We will all be busy enough for the next three years, never off duty, so relax now and have a break." But for me, that wasn't the point – I was determined to do this to the very best of my ability. I wanted to learn the language so I could communicate with the people and understand what was being said without relying on a translator all the time. I had to pass, and pass as well as I could!

So the day of the second exam came. Typical of me, I arrived at least 45 minutes early so having parked my car I nervously paced up and down the parking lot. I wondered who the Albanian examiner would be. I had been briefed that there would be one examiner representing the university and he wouldn't speak the language, and an Albanian. Everything would be recorded and sent back to the University. I was flicking through my vocabulary cards, then my notebook I had made with grammar rules, tenses and declensions. This is how nervous I am with exams! After the months and months of hard work that I had put in, I knew this was only making me more nervous, but I couldn't stop myself.

A car pulled in and an attractive young lady confidently got out, gathered her things, and walked to where the exam would take place. Was that the Albanian examiner? She looked Albanian! I wanted to speak to her, not for any nefarious reason but just to speak Albanian to someone to help calm my nerves and stop this ridiculous attempt at last minute cramming!

I waited another ten minutes and walked in. Sure enough, there she was, along with a man who introduced himself as the one who would be representing the University of Westminster. There were still 10 or 15 minutes before the allotted start time so whilst the man organised his papers and audio recorder, the Albanian lady offered to show me where the exam would take place, and remind me of the format. Her smile helped me relax and I started to chat quite naturally in Albanian. She stopped and stared at me. Oh my word, had I messed up already?

> *"You are speaking with a slight Shkodran accent. Have you been there? That is my home city."*

Hugely relieved I told her about my homestay and how I had come to love the city and longed to return. The ice was well and truly broken and I could relax, at least to some extent. I told her of the places I had visited and the books by Ismael Kadare I had read, titles memorized in Albanian, and she seemed bemused at my enthusiasm.

If I recall correctly, there were five parts of the exam and it was to last four hours in total. The last part of the exam came, and I was feeling much more confident. Yes, I was sure my answers hadn't been perfect and my nerves would inevitably have resulted in mistakes I wouldn't normally have made, but at least I had understood everything and felt sure that I had answered sufficiently well in the first four parts. This final hurdle was in a small room with the two invigilators facing me across a desk. The English tutor would play a recording in Albanian, then ask me a question about it in English, and I would reply in English. The Albanian lady sat next to him. He started with the first section, playing the recording. I smiled to myself – I was confident that I had understood every word. Easy! He asked the question – simple enough, I gave the answer without hesitation. He looked at his papers and then scribbled something down. Second question – same again. This time, after I confidently replied, he looked at me strangely for a second or two. I looked at the Albanian lady who leaned back in her chair so she couldn't be seen by the man and kindly gave a slight nod and smile of encouragement. Third question – again, I understood everything and replied without a pause. Again the Albanian lady gave me a slight smile. But this time the Englishman said,

"Are you sure?"

I replied that I was absolutely sure – the Albanian lady gave a very slight nod to me. But the English invigilator asked again,

"Do you want to reconsider your answer?"

Was he trying to trick me? Surely not!

"No, I gave you the correct answer. But I want to stop the exam. I feel something isn't right."

It seemed from his reaction that this had never happened before. Slightly flustered he said,

"We cannot stop the exam. This is being recorded."

I looked steadily at him and replied,

"Well, I don't mind speaking and having this recorded if you like! I am 100% confident that I have answered all the questions correctly, and yet your reactions seems to suggest that you don't think I have. If you think I have answered incorrectly, something is wrong."

I then turned to the Albanian invigilator and asked,

"Have I not answered correctly?"

She also looked confused,

"Yes you have, every answer is correct."

A brief consultation then occurred at their side of the table. It turned out that the British invigilator had been looking at the completely wrong sheet of answers and as he hadn't got a clue what the Albanian recording had been he didn't know the answers he was looking at didn't tally with the dialogue he had played! No wonder he was looking at me strangely.

They found the right sheet, compared what I had said, and we finished the exam, with the Albanian lady and I smiling to each other. I was later to meet her in Durrës when she was visiting Albania part way through my three year stint, and we shared a good laugh about this strange event.

Thankfully, when the results were announced, I had passed!

Some weeks later I was to fly to Albania for the next three years. What follows are a few of my memories and stories about this beautiful country.

PESHKOPI to FUSHE LURE
via GRYKE NOKE

I had taken a few days away from Tirana to explore another part of Albania that I hadn't as yet visited, and this tale comes from the part of the journey where I left Peshkopi and was heading for Fushë Lurë. It is certainly a beautiful area of the country but I was traveling not as a tourist, and as I only had a limited time unfortunately it meant I couldn't hang around anywhere for too long.

I should say from the outset that this was at a time when few foreigners were visiting some of the remoter places on my schedule, but as I wrote in the Introduction, personally I never felt threatened or had any problems. Whether that was because, at that time, I was speaking quite reasonable Albanian, and I had learnt as much as I could about local customs (but more of that later), or just plain luck, I cannot say for sure. Maybe a combination of factors, but also, as I have seen in just about every country where I have lived, some tend to like to exaggerate the dangers and talk up the negatives, perhaps in an attempt to make themselves seem more interesting or important! I am not suggesting that there weren't/aren't genuine risks and very real concerns and "challenges", but I am sure that those become more dangerous if one treads in ignorance or with a misguided air of pomposity, over-confidence or superiority which I saw too many foreigners assume.

Nevertheless Albanian friends, please do not think that I am a foreigner blind to the many terrible things that have happened, and continue to happen, nor the very real struggles that many suffered. For those who read the lengthy Introduction I hope I made that clear, and I am not going to repeat any of that. My aim is to tell something of my many positive experiences in this beautiful and unique country.

My view was that I was a foreigner in someone else's country, and it was therefore my responsibility to make the effort, to go the extra mile to read, observe, learn as much as I could, not expect those whose country it was to change to suit me and my background. Indeed, I feel the same in the country where I live now.   Nevertheless the Albanian traditions of hospitality repeatedly surprised me and drew me into the talons of the welcoming eagle that protected and guided me on my journeys. I became so fascinated and enamored with Albania that I growingly felt that at least a part of me must be Albanian! This feeling started from the first month I spent in my beloved Shkodra, when and where somehow I felt so much at home, a feeling which continued to increase the more I saw, and the more I learnt, about the real traditional values of the Albanian people. Such traditional values are so much richer than those warped modern misinterpretations which some use and which soil the original beauty and culture into sordid criminality which would disgust the true heroes of Albania.

Anyhow, I digress, and I apologize for repeating what I had already written in the Introduction, so now let's get to this journey.

At that time accurate maps were hard to come by. I had one readily available road map but it lacked the detail I needed for my travels off the main routes and I therefore tended to use old Albanian army sheet maps which I had come by. In the years since I left, more accurate maps have become readily available.

I would have loved to have stopped for a few days to explore Peshkopi. I groan at the "tick it off the list, been there, seen that" type of "busy tourism" which so many nowadays seem to enjoy. In my opinion, this form of travel can only give one a most rudimentary and superficial overview which can be so inaccurate as to be worse than not visiting at all. And yet how many times do such transitory visitors who spend a few days in a place make grand statements which suggest that they are somehow "experts"! As I once said to a friend whose holidays are always of that nature – the General visiting a regiment only sees what the Colonel wishes him to see, and all too often goes away believing that morale is high and everything in order, even on the eve of a mutiny! Anyhow, that was the case for me during this trip and I only managed a one-night stopover in Peshkopi.

187 kilometres from the capital city, Tirana, and a mere 20 kilometres from the border with Macedonia, Peshkopi is the main city of the district (rreth) and county (qark) of Dibër. I had read a little bit about its ancient history, at least enough to know that its first inhabitants were in the pre-Christian era. As I sat in my very simple but sufficient hotel room that night I wished I could tell all those people who know so little about Albania that in fact it is the most ancient and fascinating culture in Europe.

I vaguely remembered reading snippets of Peshkopi's history, and how it was clearly seen on 11th century maps. After the Ottoman expansion across Albania, Peshkopi became almost completely Muslim by the late 16th century, despite the Christian history of the town which had been recorded in some detail 500 years earlier. The Turks built a large barracks in the town in 1873. In 1910 the town had been active in the uprising against the Turks, fighting for independence, and the town was liberated from the Ottoman grip on 16th August 1912. But, as happened elsewhere in Albania, although the Albanians had believed that they were fighting together with the other Balkan States against a common foe, others were in fact looking to carve up the Albanian country for themselves. In December 1912 the Serbs invaded Peshkopi. Albanian groups retook the city on 20th September 1913, only for the Bulgarians to invade in January 1916. The locals bravely resisted as best they could, despite all that they had already suffered during the fights against first the Turks and then the Serbs. But this was still not the end. The Austro-Hungarians were allies of the Bulgarians and in April 1916 they deployed a force to punish the locals for resisting the Bulgarians. Houses were burned and numerous locals were executed for resisting the invaders. After the end of the First World War the Austro-Hungarians, being on the losing side, left the area in September 1918.

In 1939 the Italians invaded Albania, occupied Peshkopi by mid April, and remained in the area until they left the Axis in 1943 when Albanian Partisans then retook the town. Still Peshkopi was not at peace as Partisans fought with those of the Balli Kombëtar. These various groups are explained in a little bit more detail in the chapter, "The British in Albania During World War Two". In July 1944 German forces occupied the city, but were expelled later that same month. Fighting continued in the area for another few months until the area was dominated by the National Liberation Army (Ushtria Nacional Çlirimtare) (partisans/communists), and after the war 45 years of extreme communism followed.

I wished I could spend more time in such a fascinating place, but to really even scratch the surface of how inhabitants now felt about their troubled history would take much more than another few nights, even if I could stretch my break away from Tirana. I believe that we ignore history at our peril, but nevertheless history is not a subject to be considered in the cozy armchair of an air-conditioned study without risking misleading and meaningless conclusions. History needs to be taken in a geographical context with all possible time and cultural aspects considered. Of course the best historians do so successfully, but still to really get a feeling of the relevance of history today there is nothing like spending an extended period of time in a place with its people.

But I had no such luxury, with limited time and more places to visit. I wished to visit Fushë Lure and had been given the name of the local doctor who apparently would arrange somewhere for me to stay for a night. He was expecting me, and so after a simple but adequate breakfast it was time to look at my map and get moving again.

As my assistant and I left Peshkopi I couldn't help but think of all the fighting that had occurred across this area, how much blood had been spilt, against Turks, Serbs, Bulgarians, Austro-Hungarians, Italians and Germans, and then if that wasn't enough Albanian fighting Albanian as the different factions fought for control of the area.

I had studied my map and found what looked like an interesting route. All was going well and I was thoroughly enjoying the truly beautiful countryside. After a while the narrow road reached a junction which wasn't appearing on my old map. A group of youths were hanging around doing what, I had no idea, there was nothing there but a couple of roads, well, impacted earth tracks. My assistant was driving at the time and I told him to stop. He was much more nervous about the stories of "being careful in these remote places" and after a *"Are you sure boss?"* he gingerly brought the vehicle to a halt. I called out to the teenagers and they came over with big grins. After a couple of polite greetings I asked *"Which way is Grykë Noke?"*. They all pointed to the right, so with a *"faleminderit"* away we went towards the couple of houses a few hundred yards away, my assistant looking noticeably relieved. What he didn't notice, but I did, were the boys laughing heartily as we pulled away. I didn't add to his stress by telling him!

Past the first house, 90-degree turn right, yes, all correct according to my map, but yikes, hit the brakes! Right across the track was a huge pile of rocks. It was impossible to pass. So that was why those teenagers were laughing! There wasn't even room to turn the vehicle around unless we reversed into the land of the neighbouring house, and that I wanted to avoid unless invited. So we sat there for a minute or two whilst I looked at the map. Sure enough where those laughing teenagers were standing there was another track heading in the direction of Fushë Lurë across the mountain, but according to my old map it looked impassable to vehicles higher up. I got out of the car to look at the impossibly large pile of stones. It didn't take me long to realize that there was no way we were going any further on this small road.

The author asking for alternative routes, Fushë Lurë.

As I looked for how we could turn the vehicle around, the owner of the house next to the road appeared. I went over and introduced myself in my best Albanian, and after exchanging the traditional greetings and enquiries about health, whether we were strong, and if we were tired, I explained where I was trying to go to, and where we had come from. We chatted for a while and he enthusiastically told me that of course we could reverse into his land, but that before we left we must take some refreshments with them. So here we were, in Grykë Noke, not exactly sure which way we would be going to reach my destination, and yet invited most warmly into a complete stranger's house – yet again Albanian hospitality was melting my heart. Before I knew it we had three generations of his family all wanting to offer coffee, fruit, and *"How about some raki?"* I had brought some other types of fruit from Tirana which didn't seem to be available here, and so we shared it out, having a delightful little break with them all. I discussed with the gentleman my predicament with regards routes and he explained that the track I had seen, where the youths were probably still laughing at how they had sent these foreigners to a dead-end, was much better than it appeared on my old map and that it would safely get me to Fushë Lurë. So after a few group photos it was back in the car, friendly waves, wishes expressed for a safe journey, and away we went, back the way we came.

The author enjoying typical Albanian perfect hospitality.

90-degree turn, and there is the track junction, and there were the boys, sure enough still laughing and waving as they saw us return! I told my Assistant to stop again. He was even more reluctant than he had been the first time, but did so. I dropped the window and laughed and expressed my thanks to them, and then said in a half-serious tone of voice: "it was nice to visit old friends in the village, but now we need to get to Fushë Lurë – it is this track I think, isn't it?" Then I burst out laughing so they knew there were no hard feelings. Yes, they pointed up the hillside.

But before I knew what was happening they had opened the back door of the car and bundled in one of their friends. My assistant was nearly apoplectic, but the youth was in and the door was closed. He was grinning broadly and looked harmless enough. The other boys said with peels of laughter "he will make sure you head in the right direction". I turned to my Assistant – "the first rule when we get in the car – lock the doors". Breaking every rule. Too late!

Away we went up the hill, which increasingly looked like a mountain, but the track was no problem and, as the villager had assured me, much better than the old map had shown. I chatted away to our passenger: what was his name; where did he live; were those his friends (silly question!); he did realize this was a one way journey and we weren't returning to Grykë Noke, didn't he?; and so it went on. I was confident with my Albanian language then, but whatever I said, he just laughed. I tried using the Shkodran accent I had developed. Still nothing but laughter. What was wrong? I had just been chatting to that nice, welcoming family for an hour without problem, so why were all my attempts at friendly conversation with this young man met with nothing but laughter? Now even I was starting to worry!

Exploring the mountains.

As we reached nearly to the top of the mountain-pass our "guide", who hadn't said a word, suddenly slapped me on the shoulder and with his hands signaled that he wanted us to stop. My training kicked in and I quickly glanced around – seemed safe enough – no one else around – no ambush – nothing but fields and woods stretching out as far as the eye could see. Ok, stop. Out jumped the lad and came to the front window which I lowered with a smile. He shook my hand warmly, still laughing. I wondered what on earth was so funny. Was my Albanian really that hilariously bad afterall? I asked him if he lived near here – I was concerned about dumping him off in the middle of nowhere. He pointed to his chest, then across the fields to a distant stone house, and just before he turned to go he laughed loudly, gave a big shrug and pointed to his ears and mouth, shook his head, shrugged again and skipped happily across the field. I burst out laughing and watched him all the way to his house, as he occasionally turned to wave as if we had known each other for ever. I waved back each time and felt that I was now part of the joke rather than simply the ignorant subject of it. This happy guy couldn't hear or speak, but he could laugh, and he did so, almost continuously! And I am sure the lads who had found him a free ride up the hill from Grykë Noke were probably still laughing! My assistant was the only one not sharing the joke. He just sighed a big sigh of relief and probably swore at me under his breath!

Thankfully the small mountain road continued to be much better than my old map had suggested and we made good progress, relishing the beautiful views.

All I had was the name of the local doctor, so as we approached the village of Lurë and I saw a young guy at the side of the road smiling I asked my assistant to pull over. I dropped the window and again in my best Albanian offered my greetings. I then politely asked if he knew where the doctor might be. The grinning man approached the car and as he got close to the window to my complete surprise yanked up his shirt to reveal a huge scar crossing his stomach area. What is it with today I wondered – my Assistant looked concerned again! Was he proudly showing me the scar to illustrate what a great doctor they had in the village, or was it a warning of what might happen to me? I decided from the smile on the chap's face that it was probably the former, at least I hoped so! I wasn't quite sure how to react to this display of the doctor's handiwork, so just said "oh, very good, and where can I find the doctor?" With more smiles and a friendly wave I gathered that the doctor's house was right around the next bend. Sure enough, it was. The doctor told me that he had arranged a place for us to stay higher up in the woods, off the road but assuring me our SUV would be able to reach it he gave me clear instructions how to get there. I thanked him warmly and as we pulled away to look for the track through the woods I hoped that we could see something of the Lurë National Park and its famous 14 beautiful lakes which had existed since the Ice-Age. We passed one which I deduced was the "Lake of Flowers" and we caught glimpses of one or two others.

The track we had been sent on wove its way uphill and through the forest, but it was slow going and full of horrible small sharp stones. On we went, but it was impossible to miss the rocks and tyre eating jagged edges. Sure enough, just a few hundred metres from what was surely our destination a tyre burst. Earlier on in this particular trip, before this story started, we had already had one puncture and had been unable to get a repair or replacement tyre. We started the journey with two spares, but now this puncture meant we had nothing left in reserve. As I said earlier on, I had never had a problem, but nor was I so naïve to believe that some of the areas which I still intended to visit on this journey would not have seen too many foreigners. But we were stuck – we had no option but to use our second spare tyre and hope for the best – në duart e Zotit - in God's hands.

The owner of the impressively sturdy looking stone house saw us and came out to see what we were doing. In no time we had the spare wheel fitted and pulled over to the building which was in a picture perfect setting, atop a hill, surrounded by lush trees. The owner asked us to park right outside the window where, he said, he could keep an eye on the vehicle during the night. It was certainly remote with no other buildings in sight. It seemed that the house was designed to be some sort of hostel or hotel as there were at least 5 or 6 bedrooms, maybe more. Initially he gave us one room with 2 beds, but I have a bit of a thing about sharing and avoid it whenever I can. It took me some time to persuade him to give us two rooms, and he repeatedly told me that we would have to pay for both, and questioned why would I want to do that when there were two beds in one room? Eventually he was reassured that I understood and was prepared to pay.

He told us what time we could eat, and suggested we did so outside. I explained to him that I didn't eat meat or fish, but that anything at all, a bit of bread, some cheese if he had any, or potatoes, really anything but meat or fish, would be more than welcome. I assured him that I didn't want to cause him any additional work or concern.

We had a couple of hours before the appointed suppertime so decided we would explore part of the lush forest on foot. I didn't want to risk using the car any more than we had to, at least until we were away from that dratted sharp stone road. The forest and hills were so calm and tranquil, no noise except the occasional bird and the bubbling streams and cascading waterfalls. We walked as far as we dared go before the light started to fade and then decided we should make our way back to the house. Somehow we missed the track and there were a few moments of anxiousness as we looked around and tried to figure out our bearings. There was nothing to be seen but trees and more trees, whichever way we looked, the forest smothered us in her imposing embrace. The house was completely hidden but after working out the general direction based solely on the slope of the hills we set off again, and thankfully eventually spotted our destination just as the last glimmers of daylight slipped silently away. Somehow we had returned on a track lower than the one we thought we were on and we were a good ½ mile from where we should have been. But it was worth every step just to walk amongst those towering trees, to see and feel the cold water cascading down the hillside, and to watch the last glimmers of the light of a beautiful day gradually disappearing. European beech, silver fir, black pine, and the now very rarely seen Bosnian pine (threatened with extinction), what a glorious place. I had read that the area was still home to brown bears, lynx, wolves, martens and roe deer, but we neither saw nor heard sign of any of them. The negative point was that I was also aware that there had been considerable illegal logging and deforestation which had greatly affected the area.

I recalled the great Albanian poet Gjergj Fishta (1871-1940) famously saying

"Kush nuk ka pare Lurën, nuk ka pare Shqipërinë"
("Who has not seen Lurë has not seen Albania")

We reached the house just in time to sit outside at the big wooden table and whilst my assistant busied himself tapping away on his cell phone, I just breathed in the glorious air and gathered my thoughts from the interesting day we had experienced, smiling to myself. I then turned my attention to my plan for tomorrow.

Soon it was the appointed time for supper. What a feast. I have always taken the view that I am the troublesome one with my diet, and I never want to make a fuss although won't waver from my diet as it is for religious reasons. But even though I never met another vegetarian in my three years in Albania, the effort that always seemed to be made to provide me with a wonderful meal always amazed and frequently embarrassed me. I hope I was not too much trouble for anyone. We had byrek, bread, cheese, salad, tomato, yoghurt, fruit, coffee, and plenty of raki and beer if we wanted it.

Before I had even taken a bite a group of men suddenly arrived from the village, including the doctor who had so kindly arranged this excellent place for us to stay. It seemed that word had got out that there was this strange foreigner who seemed to speak Albanian, either that or the local men simply wished to give us a warm welcome. Perhaps both.

We chatted away and the food was scrumptious, and the raki flowed freely! I remember my assistant wasn't much taken with raki, but maybe that was a good thing as I intended on leaving at first light, and he could be fresh-headed to drive safely again. Once more Albanian hospitality was the most fabulous experience. Here we were, two foreigners, in the middle of a remote forest, and we were being treated so amazingly well. I was happy, perhaps with a slight "raki buzz", when out of the corner of my eye I saw a lady slip out from the house. She was dressed in black, head covered. I very politely called out,

> *"Oh lady, thank you so much for the lovely meal. It is delicious."*

SILENCE! Absolute SILENCE.

The whole table fell quiet and the men were all looking at each other, one to the other, as if waiting for one to speak. I instantly realized I had made a grave error in calling out to the lady. The men looked at each other, then to the house owner, then to me, then to each other. I was sure I had spoken very politely, using the honorific, but clearly something was seriously wrong. It felt like an eternity before the eldest of them exclaimed,

> *"It is alright, he is a foreigner, he doesn't know our traditions".*

He then turned to me and in a very serious voice instructed me in clear Albanian so there was no possibility of misunderstanding,

> *"You shouldn't speak to the lady of the house. If you want to comment about the meal you tell the master of the house, and if he wants to tell his wife what you said that is up to him."*

Oh my word, what a mistake! I prided myself on studying the traditions and trying my very best to respect them, and here I was behaving no better than any other tourist. I apologized profusely and was reassured that no harm was done, but I had learnt my lesson and never would be so careless again.

So that is the tale of that leg of this particular trip away from Tirana. The next day was time to head north to Kukës for another overnight stop before heading up to Bajram Curri.

Unfortunately we couldn't get the two punctured tyres fixed so I felt I had no sensible option but to curtail the rest of the journey after that. It was time to head west to my beloved Shkodra, and then south to Tirana. But that is a story for another time!

THE DAY OF OUR LADY OF SHKODRA
26th April

As the road to Shkodra turns to cross the River Buna, with the confluence with the River Drin behind it, the view of Rozafa Castle dominates the skyline with a welcome from the great city. The ancient stone walls proudly declare resilience and a warning to those of mal-intent, almost as if to say that visitors are most welcome to proceed, but be under no illusion as to our strength. And then as the road respectfully curves around the hill on which the castle is built, the splendid ochre walls of the "Church of Our Lady of Good Counsel" ("Zoja e Shkodres", or "Our Lady of Shkodra") suddenly greet us warmly. It appears to radiate compassion over the road, almost as if it to balance the symbol of warrior-strength of the castle. Whenever I see her, I feel as if I have arrived home. Rozafa Castle encourages me on my journey as it appears from miles before crossing the Buna and Drin, but the Church makes my heart smile and I know that I have arrived in my glorious Shkodra, one of the most ancient cities in the Balkans, and a beacon of art, music, culture and entertainment, and a place that grabbed my heart like no other.

This church is most famous for a single small painting, and one that is no longer even there, and without clear evidence as to when it was first seen.   The painting, measuring a modest 40 x 45 cms is of the Blessed Mother Mary holding baby Jesus, but details of who painted it are debatable. It is in fact a fresco, painted on a thin layer of plaster, supposedly no thicker than eggshell. Even though the original painting is no longer physically present in Albania, the legend lives on in the hearts of Albanian Catholics.

Shkodra held strategic importance for both the Venetians and Ottomans and had been occupied by both during its long history. But this power struggle began long before that, and yet our beloved Shkodra still survived with its own unique culture and character. In 1396 the city had been ceded to the Republic of

Venice who considered it important as protection for its trade routes, whilst the Turks saw Shkodra's importance as a stepping-stone for a march on Rome. Since the 1444 League of Lezha united Albanian clans in their resistance to Ottoman oppression, the national hero Skanderbeg and his brave soldiers had been fighting the Turks. The League collapsed just 6 years later, but nevertheless some northern areas were still holding out against the Ottomans with Venetian support. Skanderbeg died in 1468, just one year after our story occurred.

Spring of 1467 arrived with mounting gloom for the northern Albanians and from the grey walls of Rozafa Castle villages all around could be seen ablaze, burning at the hands of the invading Turks, crops destroyed, and villagers fleeing to the city in the hope of food and safety. The pressure inflicted by the Ottomans was mounting daily, and many from the city itself, as well as those desperate ones from the surrounding area, sought refuge in the castle.

According to legend, but use of the word "legend" is not to suggest that it only happened in the fictional fantasy tales of yore, says that on the Feast Day of St. Mark, April 25, 1467, a thick cloud covered our beautiful church, and at the same time a cloud also descended over an old Augustinian church in the Italian town of Genazzano, 25 miles southeast of Rome. When the clouds evaporated as quickly as they had appeared the mysterious painting had disappeared from Shkodra and miraculously appeared in Genazzano.

The church of Our Lady of Good Counsel

One more detailed version of the story is that two young men, Giorgio and De Scalvis, who were very devoted to Mother Mary as depicted in this painting, were in the church praying on this day. They fell asleep and both dreamt that the Virgin told them the painting would leave to escape from the wreckage being wreaked by the Turks, and that they would see the painting's path and must follow it, wherever that might be. They followed the painting to the small Italian town.

Some claim it disappeared from Shkodra and reappeared in Genazzano on the same day, whereas others suggest there was a gap of a few days before it was seen in the Italian church. Factually it is hard to prove either way, but personally I prefer the story that it appeared on the same day – it seems more "miraculous" and less, dare I say it, as if someone might have carried it there!

The painting appeared to be floating above a small ledge in the Genazzano church, with nothing seeming to support it physically, unexplainable in appearance and display. It is said that the bells of the old church began to ring, equally inexplicably, as did other bells of the town which melodiously peeled as if they were the accompaniment of some heavenly choir. When people incredulously saw the painting, and having witnessed the amazing events, they exclaimed that the Icon must have descended in the cloud direct from heaven and called it "La Madonna del Paradiso". Subsequently it assumed the title of the "Madonna del Buon Consiglio" ("Our Lady of Good Counsel").

The dilapidated Italian church was restored and named the "Church of Our Lady of Genazzano" in respect to the miraculous painting.

Nearly 5 centuries later the church was tragically almost destroyed during the Second World War, and yet our mysterious painting remained undamaged. Even today its display is hard to fathom as it continues to apparently float unaided by physical support.

The resting place of the painting in Genazzano became a pilgrimage site for Albanian Catholics ever since. Pope Urban VIII made a pilgrimage specifically to see the painting in 1630, as did Pope Pius IX in 1864. The original home of the painting, the church in Shkodra, also became a sacred place of veneration for Albanian Catholics which continued throughout pre-communist days, and once again today it is held dear to the Catholic community.

A restoration of the painting was carried out between 1957 and 1959. During this process it was suggested that it might have originally been part of a larger fresco, although why the rest of the fresco would have been destroyed or plastered over was not explained. Some claimed that it might have been the work of Gentile da Fabriano (c.1370 – 1427). I can see no evidence that he painted anywhere but Italy, mainly central Italy and some period in Venice, and so how did this delicate painting appear in Shkodra, even more so if it was in fact part of a larger work. In catalogues of his surviving works I have not seen our painting listed. He painted in the International Gothic school and there are similarities in the style of some works accredited to him with our painting, but a comparison with some of his most famous works such as his "Adoration of the Magi" in Florence much less so. Anyhow, whoever the artist might have been, it doesn't detract from this miraculous story.

After the collapse of communism, Pope John Paul II made a historic visit to Shkodra on 25th April 1993 (remember, it was on the 25th April that the painting had disappeared some 526 years earlier, and a copy of the legendary painting was presented to the city's cathedral by His Holiness. The Church, Zoja e Shkodres, was restored with aide from the Vatican. Pope John Paul II's 1993 visit was also historic as the last Pope who had tried to visit, Pope Pius II, died en route in 1464.

So it is, and I will not be so impudent as to offer personal opinion one way or the other regarding the wonderful legend of Zoja e Shkodres and the miraculous painting of Our Lady of Good Counsel. Suffice to say that every time I see that ochre painted church in the shadows of Rozafa Castle, my heart is inexplicable warmed and I feel that my journey is complete.

The author's painting of the church of Our Lady of Good Counsel.

I have painted a small picture of this beautiful church and it hangs on my wall now in Taiwan.

Remember that the painting appeared during the Feast Day of St Mark – my parents named me Mark. And the feast day for the Zoja e Shkodres (Lady of Shkodra) (and of Our Lady of Genazzano) is celebrated on the 26th April – my wife's birthday!

I will say no more.

CORFU to GJIROKASTER
via SARANDA
(including the Corfu Channel Incident)

We had spent a pleasant few days in Corfu and had enjoyed lazy times swimming in the warmth of the Ionnian Sea. Now looking back across to the hazy, distant mountains of Albania I could well imagine how mysterious the Land of the Eagles must have been when peering across the 35 kilometres of waters during the dark days of communism when it was very much a closed country. I was also reminded that Edward Lear had painted Albania from Corfu.

It had been a much-needed break, but part of me longed to return across that channel to my beloved Albania.

PART ONE – THE CORFU CHANNEL INCIDENT

On the final day, as I relaxed on the recliner, lost in my thoughts and daydreams, I recalled the sad event which became known as the Corfu Channel incident. This event marred relations between UK and Albania for over four decades.

Actually, there were three incidents.

The first was on the 15th May 1946 when two British Royal Navy cruisers, HMS Orion and HMS Superb, sailed southwards through the Corfu Channel en-route to Corfu, and came under fire from Albanian coastal artillery. Twelve rounds of probably 4-inch calibre ammunition were fired, but thankfully all missed the ships and there were no casualties. The British vessels did not return fire. The Albanian batteries on Limioni Hill, overlooking Saranda, were commanded by Skënder Backa who said the ships were within Albanian national waters and appeared to be moving directly towards Saranda. UK demanded an apology, with Admiral Sir Algernon Usborne Willis, Commander-in-Chief in the Mediterranean threatening to order the Flag Officer of 15th

Cruiser Squadron (of which HMS Orion was the flagship) to destroy the Albanian guns either by direct fire or by landing demolition parties,

> *"This seems such a good opportunity to teach the Albanians a lesson and to demonstrate that the British flag cannot be insulted with impunity, that I strongly urge that the above action be taken without attempting to extract an apology."*

Cooler heads prevailed in London, however, and the Admiral was told not to take such action, and that,

> *"His Majesty's Government expects an immediate and public apology from the Albanian Government for the outrageous action of the Albanian shore batteries concerned, and an assurance that the persons responsible have been severely punished. An early reply is expected."*

Without making this story too long, dear reader, allow me to attempt to summarise the next actions. The Albanian Armed Forces General Command issues an instruction through the US Mission in Tirana that all foreign warships and merchant vessels must not sail in Albanian territorial waters without prior notification and permission. The Albanian argument was that on-going territorial disputes with Greece and that Greece had made numerous provocative incursions into Albanian waters, justified the stance. Indeed, it was true that Greece continued to make claims for Albanian territory and cross border skirmishes were frequent at this time. Indeed, going off on another tangent, on the 23rd May 1946 Philip Dragoumis, Greek Under Secretary for Foreign Affairs, made a statement to the press in London about what the Greeks called "Northern Epirus". He declared that Greece sought the annexation of the area south of a line stretching from just south of Vlora across Albania to the southern corner of Lake Ohrid, including Pogradec and the island of Sazan. This was nothing new. The Greeks had been demanding parts of Albanian territory for the previous 30 years. Here is an interesting snippet from the dispatches of Sir Edward

Grey. This is a paragraph from a letter dated 25th November 1913 which Sir Edward sent to Sir F. Elliot in the Foreign Office in London. The context being that no matter what the International Commission was prepared to offer Greece, the Greek government still wanted more.

> *The Greek Minister continued to deprecate the line.*
> *I continued to repeat the advice, that Greece should accept whatever decisions the Powers came to. I added that if, five years ago, the Greeks had been told that they would get what they have now obtained and occupied, including such important things as Salonica, it would have seemed almost incredible.*

Let's return to the incident with the British warships. Albania claimed that they were clearly in her territorial waters and called it a "regrettable incident" and that the battery commander had not seen that they were British vessels and, had he have done so, certainly they would not have been fired upon! The Government of the Republic of Albania stated that she hoped that the Saranda incident "will not be considered an obstacle to the exchange of diplomatic representatives and the further strengthening of the friendship which exists between Great Britain and Albania".

The British government replied that it would not give any prior notice as this was an international highway through which all vessels had the right of innocent passage. They said that the Albanian response was unsatisfactory and naive, and should any British vessel come under fire in future, they would respond. The Albanians replied again on June 19th, repeating that the incident was regrettable and that "it was not the intention of the Albanian coastal commander at Saranda to attack or damage the ships of Great Britain, for which our people cherish sympathy and respect." And so it went on, with a third and final note from the British government, similarly rather repeating what had already been said.

With this first incident never having been properly resolved, it was therefore even more damaging to relations between the two countries when there was a second incident just a few months later. On 22nd October 1946 a Royal Navy flotilla, comprising two cruisers and two destroyers, deliberately passed north through the waters between Corfu and Albania in order to ascertain the Albanian reaction, with instructions to return fire if they came under attack. Close to the Albanian bay of Saranda in what was supposed to be a mine-free zone, one of the destroyers, *Saumarez*, struck a mine and was heavily damaged. The other destroyer, *Volage*, was ordered to tow the damaged vessel to a harbour in Corfu. Whilst doing so, it too hit a mine and both ships were heavily damaged. *Saumarez* was irrepairable. Sadly, forty-four British sailors died and forty-two were injured in this incident. It is worth mentioning that the Albanian coastal batteries did not fire and an Albanian Navy vessel had approached the scene flying an Albanian and a white flag. It seems probable that the mines had been laid by Yugoslavian minelayers at the request of Albania just two days before the incident.

The third incident occurred on 12–13 November 1946 when, under the direction of the Allied Commander-in-Chief Mediterranean, the Royal Navy carried out a mine sweeping operation in the Corfu channel. A French naval officer was onboard as an observer, and an aircraft carrier and other warships provided cover. Twenty-two mines were cut, two of which were taken to Malta for examination. The investigation showed that the mines were of German manufacture, but were free from marine growth and still had grease on their mooring cables which consequently strongly suggested they had only recently been laid.

Enver Hoxha, the communist leader, telegrammed the United Nations to complain about the British incursion into Albanian territorial waters. The British accused the Albanian government of laying the mines and demanded reparations for the first and second incidents, stating that the matter would otherwise be referred to the UN Security Council.

In the British government note to Albania, it was stated:

1. The Albanian Government will be aware that during the war of 1939–45 some hundreds of thousands of mines were laid in the waters of the Mediterranean and North-West Europe.

2. They will recall that in 1944 and 1945 the following areas of Albanian territorial waters were swept or searched by British minesweepers:

> ** Valona Bay—December 1944.*
> ** Durazzo Approaches—December 1944 - March, 1945.*
> ** North Corfu Channel—October 1944*

No objection to this action was raised by Albania or any other Power.

3. Only about 20,000 of the mines laid in the waters of the Mediterranean and North-West Europe had been swept by the end of hostilities. In order to carry out the formidable task of removing the remainder in a coordinated manner, an international organisation was set up in November 1945, by agreement between the Governments of the U.S.S.R., United States, United Kingdom and France. The objects of the organisation were:

> *(1) To use the available minesweeping forces to the best advantage for—*
> > *(a) the clearance of fishing grounds.*
> > *(b) the widening of all channels;*
> > *(c) the establishment of clear water for vessels, repairing important telegraph cable routes;*

*(d) the clearance of areas containing mines dangerous to surface shipping;
(e) the clearance of deep anti-submarine mines.*

(2)   To promulgate information about mines and mine clearance to the shipping of the world.

4.   The International Central Mine Clearance Board was composed of representatives of the four powers mentioned above. On the recommendation of the Central Board, other Powers were invited to become members of Zone Boards. Thus, the Mediterranean Zone Board consists of representatives of France, Greece, U.S.S.R., United Kingdom, United States and Yugoslavia. Certain other Governments were invited to send observers, but Albania was not so invited because she possessed no mine-sweeping forces.

In reply, on the 21st December 1946, the Albanian government denied the British allegations and instead claimed that the mines had been laid by other countries which did not wish to see a normalisation of relations between Albania and Britain. They went on to state that Greek and other nations' vessels had been seen in the area where the incidents had occurred shortly prior to the incidents.

There was no explanation as to why they had not made any attempt to stop the mines being laid or even seen other nations' vessels illegally in their waters. Nor was there an explanation as to why they had not warned the British of the mines had they known of their existence. The British government refused to accept the Albanian reply and brought the case to the International Court of Justice, which in due course awarded UK the sum of £843,947, agreeing with the British view that the Albanian explanation was at best dubious, but also stating that the mine-clearing operations undertaken by the Royal Navy, without prior agreement from the Albanians, had also been illegal.

The Albanian Government refused to pay the reparations ordered by the Court and in retaliation the British withheld 1574 kilograms of gold belonging to Albania, which had been looted by the Axis powers during World War Two and which had been retrieved by the Allies after the War and awarded back to the Albanians by a UK-US-French commission in 1948, but held in the vaults of the Bank of England.

Diplomatic Relations between Albania and Great Britain did not resume until 1991. On the 8th of May 1992, Britain and Albania made a joint statement that "Both sides expressed their regret at the Corfu Channel Incident of 22 October 1946", but it was not until 1996 that the gold was finally returned to Albania after it agreed to pay US$2,000,000 in delayed reparations.

Enver Hoxha publicly claimed that the whole episodes had been concoctions of the British so that they would have an excuse for a military operation into Saranda, and that the mines were either laid by the Germans during the War or by the British themselves. This all seems to be complete fiction and it is almost impossible to imagine that UK, still reeling from six years of World War and then dealing with the aftermath, would possibly be contemplating a military invasion of Saranda, and even less likely that they would be laying mines and blowing up their own ships.

Some experts claim to have evidence that the British ships were much closer to the coast than claimed. Indeed, in July 2009 sections from the bow of HMS Volage were discovered in what was clearly Albanian territorial waters. However, the Albanian claims that it had no knowledge of the mines seems to be doubtful. Bedri Spahiu, former general prosecutor and senior government official, on his release from prison in 1991, was adamant that the mines had been laid by the Yugoslavs on the specific request of the Albanian government in order to prevent the British from landing.

Even when I arrived in Albania in 2005, this was still a talking point, with views on all sides, and several Albanian friends arguing passionately that the British withholding such a sum of money (gold) for so long, when the country was so much in need, was inexcusable. Whether they truly believed, deep in their hearts, that the gold would have benefited the population had it have been returned to Enver Hoxha's regime, I do not know. Anyhow, the intention of this book is not to give detailed accounts of any incident, including this (or the later chapter on the role of UK in Albania during World War Two), but merely to give an overview and should a specific subject grab your interest, dear reader, I strongly urge you to read one of the more specialist books on that particular issue.

Anyhow, morning coffee overlooking the sea finished, it was time to put such depressing thoughts of war and diplomatic incidents aside and drive to the port and head home.

It was a short drive to the ferry from the Durrell bungalow which we had rented for the few days. I remembered reading Durrell's books when I was at school and the places he had written about seemed so far away, and yet here I was staying in his bungalow.

Reaching the port and waiting for the departure time, imagine the surprise when I saw a figure right in front of me, cigarette nonchalantly in hand, and who I immediately recognised as Endrit, one of my Albanian language teachers from London! He was equally amazed at the coincidence and told me that he was coming over because of family business concerning land – a common theme I was to hear many times. He later moved back permanently and we were to enjoy a few happy trips together, and more than a few coffees! He explained that even though he was going to Tirana, it was much cheaper to buy a non-stop air ticket from UK to Corfu, and then hop on the ferry to Saranda, and then a minibus ride from there up to Tirana. Of course I offered him a lift in my car, providing he didn't mind a brief stop in Gjirokastër en route. He was delighted! A comfortable air-conditioned SUV was definitely preferable, and safer, than a crowded minibus, and he hadn't been to Gjirokastër for many years, so that was also a nice diversion.

PART TWO – SARANDA

Forty minutes later our ferry arrived in Saranda, this beautiful part of Albania with its Mediterranean climate, beautiful coastline, and hills with citrus and olives growing in abundance. My friends from southern Albania (mostly living abroad, it must be said) tell me that I would hardly recognize the place now with the amount of development that has gone on in the last ten years, and the number of foreigners living there. It is also one of the most visited places in Albania, with cruise ships making port calls to give the inquisitive a glimpse of Albanian life, well, some form of Albanian life! A few hours in Saranda may give tourists another pleasant "Mediterranean experience", and there is absolutely nothing wrong with that, but as a "taste of Albania", well, it is like a different country altogether from the northern mountains I loved so much! Undoubtedly tourists would indeed experience some wonderful cafes and restaurants and the most polite and welcoming service. Also, for those with time, there are some incredible archaeological sites not too far from the city. The most famous of these is Butrint. Visit – you won't regret it!

As with many places in Albania, the surface impression hides an ancient and often complicated, history. Saranda had been a port town of Epirus in ancient times, with the name Onchesmus or Onchesmos. Bronze-age tools dating back to c.1400-1100BC have been discovered. Albania's first synagogue was constructed here in the 4th or 5th century by the descendants of the first Jews who had arrived in Albania around the year 70 AD. In the 6th century a Greek Orthodox church called Agioi Saranta was built, and it was from this that the town took its name.

It is believed that the city was raided by the Ostrogoths in 551AD, and also became a target for pirate raids. The Ostrogoths were a Roman-Germanic people who created one of the two great Gothic kingdoms of the Roman Empire, based on the sizeable Gothic populations who settled in the Balkans in the 4th Century AD.

By the early to mid-19th century it seems that Saranda consisted of little more than a harbor without permanent residents. In 1867, the Ottomans began to improve the port and make the area more economically independent, and so created the Saranda müdürluk (independent unit).

1877-78 saw the Russo-Turkish War, and elements in Greece saw it as an opportunity to revolt against the Ottomans, and 150 Epirote guerilla fighters landed in the Saranda region. They were soon joined by approximately 700 more volunteers, mainly Epirote refugees from Corfu, and they succeeded in gaining control of Saranda and the surrounding regions. The Ottoman military commander from Yannina, with 6,000 regular troops, supported by irregular groups of Albanian fighters, launched a successful offensive to recapture the area. In reprisal, 20 villages in the region of Delvine were burned and all escape routes were blocked, even for the unarmed civilian populace.

On the 8th October 1912 the First Balkan War began and Greek troops once again occupied Saranda. In a nutshell, the Greeks had seized the area from the Turks in the First Balkan War, but with Albania's declared independence on 28th November 1912, recognized by the Treaty of London on 29th July 1913, the area was designated as part of the Albanian State. It was claimed at the time that the Greeks living in the area refused to accept this ruling, but contemporary reports, including those of Edith Durham, clearly stated that this was not the case and that the resistance was actually organised from within Greek, and with Greek citizens, with influence from the Greek Bishop. Greece denied that was the case. The same happened in other areas of southern Albania. For example, in Christo Dako's seminal work, "Albania – The Master Key to the Near East", first published in 1919, he wrote of a similar situation in Korça in March 1914:

Thus ended the attack upon Kortcha (sic) which the Greeks claimed was a civil uprising against the inclusion of the province within the limits of independent Albania. Yet there is conclusive proof that the attack was engineered and executed by officers and men of the Greek army operating in conjunction with the Greek Bishop. The failure of this attack demonstrated the futility of the Greek argument that Kortcha (sic) is a Greek city, for the attack was repulsed by the civil population and not instigated by them.

The failure to prove Kortcha (sic) a Greek province by this means did not deter the Greeks from continuing their attacks, however, and for several months the Greek army hammered at the frontier, bombarding the whole province from three sides with long-range field pieces.

Edith Durham's accounts written during her visit to Saranda at this time were very similar. As were accounts written by officials from the Great Powers who visited Albania when considering where international borders should be drawn. The dispatches of Sir Edward Grey are littered with examples. Here are a couple of examples. First, part of a letter from the Console-General Lamb to Sir Edward Grey, Vallona [Vlora] October the 25th 1913:

Sir, ever since my arrival in this place, innumerable complaints have continued to reach me concerning the acts of injustice, violence, and pillage. committed by the Greeks, to the detriment of the Mussulman population, in the districts occupied by them in Southern Albania.

Though not attaining to the degree of savagery, of which the Serbs are accused on the eastern border, for which, indeed, they have not had even a Servians pretext of "attempted insurrection," the Greeks seem to have resorted to every means, short of wholesale murder, in order to terrorize and reduce to silence all that part of the population which they have found themselves unable by other methods to convince of its purely "Hellenic" origin and sympathies. Their action is all the more cynical and inexcusable in that it is being carried on in districts lying beyond the frontier definitely alloted to Greece by the decisions of London, and its patent object is to blot out all signs of a non-Hellenic population (in a region which ethnologically at least, is almost purely Albanian) before the arrival of the Frontier Commission.

......[the letter continues] *Whilst necessarily unable to verify the statements contained therein, I have practically no doubt of their veracity. Similar conduct has been systematically resorted to by the Greek authorities at Koritza ever since their first occupation of that place."*

[Signed] *Harry H Lamb*

This continued unabated, no matter what was said. In a letter dated 6th February 1914 Consul-General Lamb wrote Sir Edward Gray from Valone (Vlora) as follows:

Sir, in continuation of the despatch No. 26 addressed to you yesterday by Mr. Harris, I have the honor to inform you that, according to reports received here from both private and official sources, the Greek attacks upon the Albanian villages on both sides of the border line are still continuing.

On Sunday, the 2nd instant, a Greek detachment approaching the large Mussulman village of Bolena proceeded to arrest a shepherd whom they encountered on its outskirts. The latter having attempted to resist was shot down. Three other shepherds who were grazing their flocks somewhat nearer to the village, and who were witnesses of the murder, seem to have fired on the Greeks (whether before or after they had themselves been fired on is not quite clear). Two of them were killed and the other wounded by the Greeks, who are now reported to have entirely destroyed the village by fire.

Again, this completely tallies with other contemporary witness reports, including Edith Durham who also wrote of whole villages being destroyed. Anyhow, as officially the Greek military pulled back to the new internationally recognized border, they declared this to be an autonomous republic. I used the word "officially" because some contemporary reports stated that in fact many Greek soldiers remained behind to be put into action once again at a time chosen by the Greek government. Perhaps surprisingly, the Great Powers recognized that the population should be able to have its own administration and self-government, under nominal Albanian sovereignty. However, it was never implemented because the Albanian government collapsed in August 1914, and in October, following the outbreak of the First World War, the Greeks once again occupied the city.

The Italians then occupied the area between 1916 and 1920, and thus it became part of the so-called Italian Protectorate.

Greece was defeated in the Greek-Turkish war of 1919-22, and so any ideas of claiming territorial rights after the war were dissipated. The area was finally fully ceded to Albania in November 1921. Greek claims for Albanian territory continued however, as mentioned in the previous section of this chapter

Are you confused yet, dear reader? I am attempting to pull out the highlights of this complicated story, but in doing so I am all too aware that I may be skimming over things which deserve mention.

Improvements were continuously made to the port facilities until the outbreak of the Second World War and the invasion of Albania by the Italians in 1939, who used the port during their invasion into Greece. The Greeks pushed back however, and the port once again came under their control as they gained territory northwards. After the Germans invaded Greece they were forced to retreat and the city, yet again, came under Italian control.

It is worth noting, as I have alluded to elsewhere in this book, that Albanian territory had been under threat from all around, especially since the demise of the Ottoman Empire, with intentions of carving up the whole country between Serbs, Bulgarians, and Greeks. Italians, Austrians and Russians had also been playing their parts, and others including the French (in Korçe) had joined in the game.

As mentioned in the chapter, *The British in Albania During World War Two*, a small group of British Royal Marine Commandos coordinated with a group of partisans from the area and captured the town on the 9th October 1944. Knowing of the British government's affection for Greece, the partisans had feared that the intention was to re-install Greek control, but this proved not to have been the case and having ousted the Italians the British quickly withdrew, leaving the area back in the hands of the Albanians.

It was time to get on with our journey, so let us leave this complicated discussion of history to a halt for now. I was determined to visit Gjirokastër on the way back home, so it was time to get moving.

Oh, but this area's history is so rich, and as we left the city I remembered reading that some northern Albanians had settled in the area during the communist era, but whether this was voluntary or forced relocation I was unsure. The Greek Orthodox Church of St. Spyridon in the centre of the city had been destroyed by the communists, as had so many other churches and mosques. A small shrine had been built in 1991 at the site where the church had once stood. Coincidently, the remains of Saint Spyridon are placed in a church in Corfu, from where we had just come that morning.

PART THREE - GJIROKASTËR

We took the road past Delvine, travelling roughly north-east almost to the Greek border, and then north-west to Gjirokastër. I had visited a couple of times previously but it is such a beautiful and picturesque city I was keen to see it again, even if for nothing more than a very brief stop and walk around the castle, and it really wasn't far out of our way to make this detour.

Located 300 metres above sea-level, in a valley between the Gjerë mountains and the river Drina, Gjirokastër old town is an UNESCO World Heritage site. The castle towers over the city and commands incredible views in all directions – the perfect defensive fortress. I took some photographs looking across to the old town – the same view depicted on untold numbers of postcards, and I was later to paint the town from one of these snaps. The painting was bought by a Taiwanese lady, so I modestly claim to have spread a little piece of Albania the other side of the world!

The former communist leader, Enver Hoxha was born in this city, but much more appealing to me was that it was also the birthplace of my favourite Albanian author, Ismail Kadare – the one whose books I had discussed prior to my language exam, to the surprise of my Albanian examiner. To me, like Shkodra in the north, there is a feeling of culture and art in the city and sometime I would love to spend more time there, exploring in more detail, but not this visit! My friend hadn't been there for years, but we needed to get moving north so it was straight to the castle for those amazing views and just to get the briefest impression of the place.

Greek written records mention it in 1336 by its Greek name, *Argyrokastro*, but actually, the city walls can be dated back to the 3rd century. It fell under Ottoman rule for five centuries, from 1417 until 1913, and most of the buildings were built between the 17th and 18th centuries. The Turks called it Ergiri Kasri. As in much of Albania, the Ottoman period saw the conversion of a considerable percentage of the population to Islam, for various reasons, and interestingly the city also became an important centre for the Bektashi Sufis.

During the Balkan Wars of 1912–3 the city fell to the Greeks before becoming incorporated wholly into Albania after independence from the Ottomans was declared. The local Greek population rebelled against this and after several months of guerilla warfare, the short-lived autonomous Republic of Northern Epirus was declared in 1914, as already mentioned, with Gjirokastër as its capital. As with Saranda, it was finally declared to be part of Albania in 1921.

Sadly, it must be mentioned that the city was one of the major cities most embroiled in the anarchy of 1997, the subject of which is way beyond the scope of this chapter and deserves a book on its own. I will not even attempt to summarise that dark period in recent Albanian history as in doing so one must simplify, and such were the complexities that to simplify with accuracy and without showing favour would be incredibly challenging for a book such as this.

Thankfully, and very unusually in Albania, old Gjirokastër did not suffer the indiscriminate concrete "modernizing" programmes so loved by the communist regime of the 1960s and 70s. Along with Berat, it was declared a "museum town", and was formally listed as a UNESCO World Heritage site in 2005, coincidentally the year I arrived in Albania.

As we walked around the walls of the castle, as a military man I could appreciate the perfect strategic position, with panoramic views across the "City of Stone" to the hills and along the river valley beyond. It would take a skillful opponent to reach the city without being seen! My thoughts were on the periods of Albanian history hundreds of years past as we walked around the walls, looking over vistas which looked like they hadn't changed for centuries.

More ominously, it was later used as a prison and some of the rooms used as cells and torture chambers by both the Nazis and then the communist regime until 1963. For such an ancient place, in my opinion the various pieces of captured artillery and memorabilia of the Communist resistance against German occupation seemed a tad incongruous, but even more so when we came across the remains of a United States Air Force Lockheed T-33 Shooting Star aircraft. However, I was to learn that this was in fact part of the National Armaments Museum. Yet, as I readjusted my mind I recognized that this was just as much part of the history of the area as was anything else. Maybe it was the positioning of them within the castle walls which personally I found to be a distraction to my mind's imaginings of ancient battles.

I was aware that this ancient city also has an Ottoman bazaar, indeed it is one of the best preserved of its ilk in the Balkans. It was built in the 17th century and rebuilt 200 years later after a fire, but sadly time was ticking along far too quickly and I knew we had to get back on the road north. 500 homes are preserved in the city, and splendid they look too. No wonder that the likes of Byron and Edward Lear visited this beautiful place.

It was yet another of those Albanian days when I was lost in so many thoughts of the history of this ancient land, of battles and incursions, territorial disputes and more powerful neighbours bullying, and yet somehow Albanian culture remained in tact despite all attempts to obliterate it.

I guess we have to quote dates and specific events and I hope that I am finding the right balance of not too much yet not too little and that I haven't bored you with all of this, dear reader, for without these to provide some sort of framework, something onto which one can proverbially hang one's hat, it is difficult to give an impression of the depth and complexities of the places described.

As I have said elsewhere in this modest book, discussion of history, however, does not mean to suggest that things mustn't move forward – they absolutely must. Don't forget that what we do today is tomorrow's history. Nevertheless, it is through at least some understanding of where we have collectively come from, over centuries, the different cultures that have influenced events, the changes of politics, religions, and wars that have been fought and the blood spilt on the ground on which we walk that we can better understand who we are today.

This was one of those beautiful days which far surpassed all that I have described above. It was not about history, invasions, wars, politics, dates or names, nor was it a day of superficial touristy photos, it was one of those idyllic days when I just felt part of this place, part of this land and its people, however implausible that statement might seem.

It just "was".

THE BRIBE

This is a true story of a very close friend of mine who, for obvious reasons, I will not name. Please don't think I am breaking my promise of a positive book – things such as this could happen anywhere. I thought about disappearing off on one of my tangents to recount a personal experience here in Taiwan, but I will resist as I have already mentioned some such events in the lengthy introduction. My point is simply to ask you, dear reader, to pause for a moment before adding this to the negative stories about this country I love – it could happen anywhere, and I tell it here because, rightly or wrongly, it amused me, and I hope it will make you smile too.

Let's get on with this short story. This friend was one of the many Albanians living abroad – there are more Albanians living outside the country than in. This charming fellow studied at a university in UK and then entered a respected profession. He didn't work in an area of England where there were many Albanians and, as far as I am aware, the majority of his university and professional friends and associates were British. One could therefore certainly say that his post-high school years were more influenced by British culture than Albanian.

He had some family back in his country of birth however, and they, like so many others, became embroiled in legal battles over land ownership. My friend therefore decided to return "home" to take up the cudgel, figuratively speaking of course.

We met quite a few times and it was always interesting for me to hear his views. He was an intelligent man who had grown up in Albania, had a good knowledge of Albanian history, and had been active during the downfall of the communist regime. He had managed to be one of the first to move abroad, climbing aboard a ship to sail to Italy, as so many others did, and that is a fascinating insight as to the feelings at that time and the risks people were prepared to take, but irrelevant to this tale. More relevant is to repeat that he spent quite a number of important years of his life studying and then working in England. I think it is fair to say therefore that he was returning to his motherland with British views firmly implanted, the idea of "fair play" so often heard in UK, and (at least initially) idealistic intentions of helping Albanian society to continue its path to full democracy and away from corruption and "shady business".

We met one day in Durres and as we sat having a cold beer in one of the cafes I now miss so much, he told me that he had had quite an experience that week.

He had bought a secondhand car not long after he had returned in Albania. During the previous week he had been pulled over for a random police check whilst he was driving north of Tirana to look at a piece of family land. Being a fine young man who wanted to do everything "right", he was genuinely shocked and dismayed when the traffic policeman pointed out that his insurance had expired literally the day before. My friend was very apologetic – this was not at all like him and it was truly a mistake.

The policeman started to make a huge fuss, going round the car and threatening that he would issue tickets for all sorts of other minor misdemeanors, and these could be added to the "crime". My friend said that the policeman wasn't even subtle that a "contribution" for a "cup of coffee" could make the whole thing disappear and he would be on his way. But, still full of ideological determination my friend refused. He admitted that he had done wrong, but equally suggested to the policeman not to try to concoct any fictional crimes as he was recording the whole incident.

The policeman informed my friend that he could therefore not allow the car to be driven without insurance, and that he would call for a tow truck and have the car impounded and the costs of this would all have to be paid by my friend in addition to the fine for not having valid insurance, unless..... But still my principled friend refused to offer a bribe. So it was.

My friend told me it was an expensive mistake, but he had done wrong, and he felt it was only right that he should pay the fine and other bills as legally required. If he did otherwise, he believed, he would be no better than those he criticized. Corruption is corruption, no matter at what level. He told me that at least he could sleep at night knowing that he had not succumbed to the easy path of paying a bribe, however small.

The very next day my friend arranged insurance and then went to pay the fine, which now included the tow fee, the impound fee, as well as the original fine. He was told where his car had been taken to, and given the relevant paperwork to have the car released. Still feeling pleased with himself for doing the right thing he went to the car impound yard, produced the paperwork, signed whatever it was that needed signing, and was pointed to his car. With a smile of self-satisfaction, knowing he had "done the right thing" he went to collect it, only to find there was no key! He went back to the office where he had dropped off the paperwork and signed the forms and asked for the key. The grumpy guy just shrugged and continued to flick his cigarette ash onto the floor, and rustled his newspaper. My friend asked again, and again got no reply.

Dear reader, perhaps you can guess the ending. My friend had to "offer" the corrupt guy in the impound yard the same amount of money he could have slipped to the policeman in the first place, "something for a coffee", and avoided the fine and all the hassle. Needless to say, my friend was truly greatly saddened that despite all his efforts to play a "fair game", in the end the corrupt system had beaten him.

Of course I was totally and completely on my friend's side, he had tried so hard not to lower his standards, but I couldn't help but laugh, a sad and tragic laugh, but laugh I did.

A VISIT TO BERATI
WITH ARSI

Arsi was a taxi driver in Tirana. She was completely reliable, dependable and a very capable driver. She never once let us down. She did have a habit of singing extremely loudly with the windows fully open, with seemingly not a care in the world, but hey, that was one way to learn some popular Albanian pop songs. We knew the coffee shop where she hung out when she was between jobs and sometimes if we saw her sitting there when we were walking by we would pop in and have a Turkish coffee with her, and occasionally a glass of raki. Without exception we would always laugh and joke and leave happier than when we entered.....and I don't mean because of the alcohol! She was just one of those people – full of bubbly and positive energy, no matter what.

Arsi became more than our trusted taxi driver. She was one of those people I would call a friend. If that phrase sounds odd, and I suppose it does, it is because I have a reticence to throw that word, "friend", around as frequently as most seem to do. Most are "acquaintances". To me a "friend" doesn't necessarily mean that we have to go to parties together or spend time chatting every day. In my own definition a "friend" is someone I feel I can trust with complete confidence, and someone I could turn to if needed, and if they would help they would, and equally if they could not help they would say so. And of course the feeling should be mutual. Honesty, trustworthiness, truthfulness is more important to me than attending parties and suchlike. It must be said however, that I developed more "friendships" in Albania than anywhere else I have ever lived. Yes, often it took time to develop those relationships, but I think that is how it should be. Perhaps it should be said that in the sort of employment I was in, there was always a little bit of looking over one's shoulder and questioning motives, and all that. On more than one occasion I found my conversations with one person being recorded by a third party, and I found a recording device in my house, but that is all part of the game! I am sure it took some time for some people to understand that I was not one for playing games, using people, or being dishonest, as I mentioned in the introduction. What I said, I meant, and if I said I would try to do something, I really would. And I expected the same in reverse. But once such understanding has developed and has been proven over time, the relationships can be so much stronger than those formed through talking in riddles and hiding one's true intentions, because one is then left never quite sure when the games have ended and sincerity has begun. Anyhow, I digress!

One funny aside was when my wife was with Arsi in the centre of Tirana. Some young chap on a bicycle collided with the front of her taxi and down he went. Apparently without even pausing for breath Arsi leapt from the taxi, told the poor guy to get up, gave him a cigarette and an aspirin, told him to be more careful in future, jumped back in the car and drove off, with the radio at full blast as was her norm!

We came to know something of Arsi's life, and met her daughter, Rovena, who was equally delightful. One day Arsi suggested we all go out for the day, with her and her daughter, and she would drive. Well, why not. A date was fixed.

It was a hot summer's day when we met, and Arsi was in full vocal spirit, singing out of the car window at full volume as we left Tirana and headed southwards. First stop was to a beach at Divjakë, in the county of Fier. It was a lovely beach, away from the packed beaches of Durres with which I was more familiar. Arsi had relatives who owned a beachside restaurant there. We played on the sand and I needed no encouragement to run into the sea for a swim. Rovena gingerly waded out and explained that she couldn't swim. The sea was so calm and beautiful and I was sure that I could help her at least gain some confidence and so gently holding her back I told her to trust me and lay back in the soothing water, and in no time she was floating. I remember how thrilled she was. We spent some more time playing in the sea before being called back to the beach and to the restaurant for lunch. I cannot remember what was on the menu, I am sure it must have been some forms of seafood, but for me as a vegetarian it was the usual delicious fresh salad, cheese and bread, of which I never tired.

It was just one of those beautiful times, just the four of us, no work, no politics, just warm sunshine and equally warm feelings of friendship. I could have happily stayed on the beach all day, but after lunch Arsi announced that we were going to Berat. I had visited a few times in the past, but it is one of those magical places of which I could never be bored.

And so it was back into Arsi's car and head inland, eastwards, to this beautiful UNESCO World Heritage Site of Berat, about 70kms south of Tirana.   It felt good to be spending a day not in my official car, nor my CD-plated private car, but just relaxing with two lovely people who wanted nothing from me, and I wanted nothing from them, just friendship and making happy memories.

We crossed the river Osum not far from where it is joined by the river Molisht. What a beautiful place, framed by pine forests and the Tomorr mountains beyond, the town rises from the gorge carved out over time by the river. On one side of the river is the part of the city called Gorica, and then Mangalem at the foot of the hill which then towers over the rest with the area known as the Kalaja, or castle, as the crowning glory. The architecture is simply wonderful, a feast for the eyes, and set in such wonderful natural beauty that it is the stuff of fairytales.

And talking of fairytales, as we approached the hill I recalled an old Albanian legend which said that the Tomorr mountain was originally a giant who had battled with another giant mountain called Shpirag. Needless to say the battle was over a beautiful young woman. Both giants died and all that was left of them were the two mountains. The girl over whom they had fought burst into such floods of tears that she drowned in them. Her tears became the river Osum!

Arsi parked her car and the four of us walked into the walled castle area. I was keen to explore and learn more of the history of the place. It was a hot day however, and having spent so many hours in an un-air-conditioned car, and then hours on the beach, one of our small group's tempers was getting frayed – I won't say whose, but it wasn't mine, Arsi's or Rovena's! My phone rang, and I cursed it, always on call, but that goes with the job, and it was an easy fix. Back to exploring Berati and balancing the time I wanted to spend there with the other's shortening temper!

Beautiful and ancient Berat.

There were records of inhabitants in the city since at least the 6th century BC, yes dear reader, over 2,600 years. According to one guidebook I had read the earliest settlers were an ancient Greek tribe of the Dassaretae or Dexarioi, a subgroup of the Chaonians. I couldn't help but wonder if Albanian historians would agree with this as Albanian culture dates back to the Ilyrians, pre-Greek and Roman and I recalled reading previously that in fact there were inhabitants here since the Bronze Age, 4000 years ago! Something for further study at some time. The city was captured by the Romans in 200 BC, and the walls were destroyed and the male population massacred. It then had a very mixed and complicated history after the fall of the western Roman Empire, with repeated invasions by Slavs.

During the Roman and early Byzantine period, the city was known as *Pulcheriopolis*. Then the Bulgarians captured the town in the 9th century, and it was not until the years of the Ottoman rule that the city's name was changed to Berat. From the 11th century for the next 500 years or so the history became even more complicated with repeated attacks and changes of rulership, and this is all deserving of a book on its own.

I tried to flick through the pages of a guidebook I had brought with me, but it was clear that I was pushing my luck with the patience of one of our small group in the hot afternoon sun. Not wanting to spoil the lovely atmosphere of this beautiful day I put the guidebook in my bag and decided to soak up what was before my eyes instead. I could read a guidebook anytime!

Of course the 13th century Byzantine Holy Trinity Church, incredibly one of eight churches within the citadel, was a highlight and must-have photo stop.

OK, a bit more history - in 1417 the town was under Ottoman control, and despite a failed attempt in 1455 by the national hero Skanderbeg, with an Albanian force of 14,000 to dislodge the 40,000 strong Ottoman defenders, it remained under Ottoman control for the next 500 years. A period of decline accompanied the early Ottoman days, and by the end of the 16th century records show only 710 houses remained in the city. The following 100 years showed a recovery, however, and it became a major arts and crafts centre, with woodcarving especially highly developed. By the 18th century it was again one of the most important cities in Albania.

Berat also developed into a major centre of support for the

League of Prizren – the famous late 19ᵗʰ century Albanian nationalist alliance.

At least 60 Jewish families were concealed in Berat from persecution during World War Two. As an aside, Albania was the only country in continental Europe which had a larger Jewish population after the War than before, and the story of the Albanian people's sheltering of the Jewish migrants, often at considerable personal risk, is in itself an amazing story which illustrates the incredible traditional Albanian culture of looking after and protecting guests. As the very famous Albanian saying goes, "The home belongs to God and the guest."

I could have happily stayed on the beach all day, and now I felt that I could have stayed in Berat for the rest of the day, exploring, hearing stories, learning, looking, and just soaking up the atmosphere, but I had pushed my luck over how much one of our party would take! It was time to move on and probably to find an air-conditioned restaurant on the long drive back to Tirana. As we walked along the narrow streets and looked over the tiled roofs to the town below and the distant mountains I could imagine how little things had changed over the centuries, and yet how much this city had seen and suffered. My imagination ran riot as I thought how wonderful it would be if the local population accepted me at some future time and how I would love to have a small art studio here.

Some years later, long after I had left the country, I saw an advertisement for a wonderful old house for sale within the old area of the town, in dire need of restoration as far as I could ascertain from the photographs. I spent many an evening day-dreaming that "this could be mine", envisioning how I would strive for a sympathetic restoration, returning it to its former glory but sensitively without destroying its character, and with solid wood furniture hand carved by Albanian craftsmen rather than imported Italian store bought stuff usually seen, and traditional hand-woven Albanian carpets on the old stone floors, and my imagination raged on. In my imagination I could envisage traditional Albanian musicians, artists and writers visiting regularly, with art exhibitions and displays of the best local handicrafts, and impromptu gatherings with musicians playing lutes and çifteli, and polyphonic singing. Sadly, the asking price was, in my opinion, way beyond what was realistic for a house that looked from the photographs like it was ready to crumble if not saved soon.....but what do I know! I hope someone else has now bought it and doing the needful.

We made our way home, all relaxed, tanned from the sun, and happy with each other's company. As Rovena and Estella took a nap in the back seat I kept Arsi company in the front. Inevitably she knew the perfect restaurant which would make a break in the journey and as was always the case in Albania the hospitality was perfect and the food healthy and fresh.

The rest of the journey was uneventful and Arsi's excellent driving skills delivered us safely home, tired but happy, and another part of Albania explored. I would return to Berati several times more and would love to visit again now. I hope it hasn't changed too much – somehow I have the feeling that the people of the town sufficiently understand the beauty and uniqueness of what they have to ensure that it is not spoiled by short-term and short-sighted development. If you have the opportunity to visit, do so, and if you come across a foreigner with a small art studio say hello – it could be me!

MY VERY GOOD FRIEND
ZOTI RIZA LAHI

I am making an exception to my self-imposed restriction not to write in this small book about people I met through my work, but I am sure that my very good friend, the late Zoti Riza Lahi, would give me his approval.

Riza was born in Shkodra on the 16th January 1950. On the 31st December 2013, as I sat in my toom in Taiwan, I heard the tragic news that he had suddenly passed away in Tirana. It was a great shock to me. Riza and I had stayed in touch with each other even after I left Albania and spent 3 years in Nepal, and then when I deployed to Afghanistan for 6 months, before taking retirement and settling in Taiwan – we still exchanged emails, still had loose plans for projects together, still shared dreams and ideas. I offer this essay to you dear Riza, I hope it would make you smile and laugh in that infectious way you always did, with a mischievous sparkle in your eyes.

How I first met Riza is a story which must be told.

I was fairly new into my appointment as the British Defence Attaché in Tirana when I received a telephone call from the Albanian Ministry of Defence's press office. The conversation went something like this, translated:

> *"Hello, my name is Riza Lahi. I have already heard so much about you...."*

Me:

> *"Really?"*

(thinking to myself, 'I wonder what, and by whom, good or bad! Where is this conversation going?')

Riza:

> *"Yes, and I am wanting to start a new series of articles in our in-house Ministry of Defence magazine about the foreign Defence Attachés."*

Me, uncommittedly:

> *"Uh huh"*

(remembering all the warnings I had been given in my lengthy pre-deployment training about being careful with journalists and any quotable comments.)

Riza:

> *"Yes, and I have heard so much about you and I want the very first article to be about you, an interview. It will be so wonderful. Can we meet for coffee?"*

Me (nervous!):

> *"Yes, of course, ok, where and when?"*

As was often the case in Albania, we agreed to meet not in the office but in a coffee shop. Riza spotted me and shuffled over, twinkle in his eyes, big grin on his face, as if we were old friends, shaking my hand vigorously and kissing both cheeks! We had a pleasant coffee over which we chatted about things in general. I learnt that Riza had been a MiG pilot in his younger days and I still have a photo of him as a young man, sat in his aircraft. I have kept meaning to draw that portrait as a memory of him – one day I will do so. I explained that I had to be careful what I said in any interview, but Riza was so bubbly and enthusiastic it was hard to refuse him, and afterall, this was an official Albanian Ministry of Defence magazine, and the interview would be with Riza, ex-pilot and now writer and poet, so surely he would understand the sensitivities. We agreed a date.

The interview took place, with me remembering all my training and being extremely careful not to say anything which could be misconstrued, potentially embarrassing, misleading, or untrue. I reminded Riza that I must see the draft before it went to print, and that was my firm condition. He agreed, "Of course", and that lovely warm smile again, and handshake, and hug, and kiss on both cheeks.

A couple of weeks passed and then one beautiful Albanian morning my secretary brought in the latest copy of the Ministry of Defence magazine. Yes, you guessed it, there was, *"Interview with the British Defence Attache, Lieutenant Colonel Mark D. Vickers"*. WHAT? I nearly fell off my chair and hit the roof at the same time, if that's possible. I was supposed to see and agree the draft. I quickly found the relevant pages and read through it. There was much I hadn't said, but harmless, so far so good. But then, *"Lieutenant Colonel Vickers declared that to show his love for our country he was optimistic that he would persuade UK to donate a fleet of helicopters......."* My jaw must have almost hit the table.

I shouted to my secretary,

"Ardiana, get Riza Lahi on the phone IMMEDIATELY"

Oh boy oh boy.

"Riza – you promised to show me the draft, and why have you changed so much of what I said. And helicopters? We never even mentioned helicopters and there is not a hope that I could ever achieve something like that......."

Before I could say more, Riza's cheery and unperturbed interjection:

"Oh Colonel but isn't it wonderful? Doesn't it read so nicely, so poetic, so beautiful. I thought it would be a lovely surprise for you ....."

"Riza – HELICOPTERS?"

"Oh Colonel, you don't understand. Of course we know you won't do that, but it shows how much you love our country. It shows how hard you want to work and how you care about us..."

"Riza....NO....no helicopters, no changing my words, no poetry...this is a disaster. If my Ambassador reads that, or somehow someone back in London, I could be finished here. I demand you print a full retraction and apology. Goodbye."

A day or two later I was still fuming, but somehow Riza was such a likeable character that a small, very small, part of me was also laughing at his audacity. So poetic indeed! He had obviously taken my final comments to heart before I slammed the phone down on him, and the jungle drums were beating and I heard that he was potentially in very serious trouble. I intervened on his behalf. I was still livid but I didn't want him to lose his job. I pleaded his case. He remained, and we became great friends.

Skip forward another month or two and Riza calls again.

"Colonel, I have a wonderful idea. How would you like to have supper with the President and me?"

Gosh, an informal supper with the President? I wasn't sure what my Ambassador would say, but surely this was an opportunity I mustn't miss. And what a regain, Riza, after the "helicopter" debacle – from our last encounter to this – supper with the President! Well done Riza! Well done my friend. I was so surprised.

"Oh that would indeed be wonderful Riza. Tell me the date and time and I will clear the diary, no matter when. Of course I will be there."

Riza:

"Well, I have already spoken to the President and suggested a restaurant out in the country where you might not have been before. How about Thursday?"

"Of course, wonderful, thank you so much Riza. Will anyone else be there?"

I was somewhat surprised Riza was on such personal terms with the President of Albania that we could share such an intimate supper together. I knew I should tell my Ambassador, but then he might stop me going alone. Should I wait and tell him afterwards?

"Well, I will get someone to drive us so that you can have a drink. You can bring your wife if you like. So it will be just us..... and the President of the Roma community. We have been friends for a long time."

What? Did I just hear that correct? President of the ROMA community? Not the President as in "President". Oh Riza! Me, perhaps sounding slightly less excited:

"Errr, yes, ok, err, fine, see you then, end of the Embassy road at 7pm."

So it was, and actually I became quite excited at the prospect, even though it wasn't actually the same President I thought we were going to meet! Riza and his driver picked us up. It was a dark Autumn night and the clouds burst open in a torrential downpour. As we left Tirana on a pot-holed road I had never travelled, with the old Benz's suspension crashing and banging, in pitch blackness with no street lights and hardly another car in sight.   The headlights of the tired Mercedes struggling to illuminate the road even a few meters ahead, thoughts of all my careful and extensive Attaché training flooded my mind as Estella nervously gripped my hand and gave me a look as if it say "What have you got us into?" She was clearly scared. What am I doing here? Am I safe? Where am I going? No one knows where I am and phone coverage keeps cutting in and out. But needless to say my worries were groundless.   After an hour, which seemed much longer, the car swung off the road and into the deserted car park of a typically lovely Albanian country restaurant – the sort of place I came to love so much in Albania.

Food and drink were ordered and we chatted in Albanian as if we had known each other for years. The company was as warm as the glorious log fire. The President (of the Roma Community!) explained to me the two main groups of Roma, one coming up from Egypt in the south and the other originally west from India. He came from the latter group. We touched on languages and I couldn't help trying out a few words of Nepali which is very similar to Hindi.   Pointing to the water jug, *"pani"* I said, to which the President nodded and said *"yes, pani"*. *"Ek, dui, tin, char, panche..."* counting on my fingers, *"yes, yes, very similar"*. I explained that I had served with the Gurkhas from Nepal years before and had spoken their language (little did I know at that time that my next appointment after Albania would be in Nepal). Laughter and slaps on the back and food and more drink. All in all it was a wonderful evening, and something I could never have enjoyed without Riza's kind, if initially confusing, invitation.

I suppose this second encounter was the start of our real friendship. We were beginning to understand each other and share jokes and dreams and ideas and hopes and smiles.

Riza presented me with one of his novels, in Albanian, which I read with relish, to his great delight.

I invited Riza to all our Embassy formal events, and to quite a number of my own less formal parties. Once I invited a couple of attachés and some of those from the Albanian Ministry of Defence who had become friends, and also Prince Leka, to a supper at a restaurant called "Sofra e Ariut", on the outskirts of Tirana, and I invited Riza along too. I clearly recall how thrilled he was to be included.

We met many times and had many, many coffees together before I left Albania three years after our first meeting.

When I was posted to Nepal we remained in contact and one day he contacted me and said that he had finished a short children's story of maybe 30 pages, and it was his dream to have it published in English. He asked if I could translate it for him. My Albanian was already getting rusty through lack of use, plus my efforts to regain the Nepali language which I had originally learnt in 1980 had damaged it further, but I promised to do the best I could.

> *"Oh good, good, thank you. I really want to see this published in English one day. Good, good."*

And so I somehow made time from my busy job to translate "A Saturday Night and a Star" into English, to the best of my ability. Thinking he would be delighted with my efforts I sent the translation back to him.

> *"Oh thank you Colonel. Good. Good. It is my dream to see this published in English....."*

(yes, I know Riza, you told me several times)

> *".....so if you can now contact some publishing houses for me."*

Oh Riza!

I did do so, but all wanted more money that I could spare and "A Saturday Night and a Star" was never published in English.

Recently, I have trawled through my old external hard drives to find that draft once more in the hope that maybe one day I could contact Riza's family and ask if they would be in agreement for me to self-publish it in his name – an option that I didn't have at that time. I feel very sad that several changes of computer later I cannot for the life of me find it. I will keep looking.

Riza was always delighted with the articles about Albania I had published in the years after I left his beautiful county. His enthusiasm was infectious. He was always thrilled with my great interest in his home city of Shkodra, and that I was known by the nickname "Marku Shkodani". Once he optimistically and excitedly declared, "I am going to speak to some of my contacts in Shkodra and I am sure they will award you with honorary Shkodran citizenship!" Needless to say it never happened – just another shared dream with my dear friend!

Another time he contacted me with another wonderful "Riza idea",

> *"Marku, why don't you buy a property in Shirokë, on the banks of the beautiful Shkodra lake. You could buy something with wonderful views of the castle and I could look after it for you. I like to walk that way everyday when I am in Shkodra and I frequently compose my poems as I walk alongside the lake. It is so beautiful. I think it is a wonderful idea."*

Yes, wonderful idea Riza, and it would be a dream come true, to own a house in Shkodra, but unaffordable!

The year before he left us we were dreamily discussing two ideas. One was typically optimistic Riza on a grand scale, to organize an Asian tour for an Albanian youth dance troupe. I said I could probably organise venues in Taiwan, but how could we afford airflights and accommodation and living expenses? Always dreaming big, he once told me,

"Marku, we must never stop dreaming, and even if we just have those dreams and ambitions but cannot fulfill them it is alright, but don't stop dreaming. One day we will sit together with a coffee in Shkodra and laugh about it."

If only we could my dear friend.

The other idea was also a dream, but at least potentially more achievable. The suggestion was for an exhibition of some of my antique prints (see elsewhere in this book) and my own paintings of Albania, to be displayed alongside some of his beautiful poems.

Some years ago I was in UK for a few days en route to Afghanistan. Riza had a newspaper with one of my articles printed and he wanted to send it to me, and a letter from Justina and Domenika from Shkodra. I asked if he could post them to my sister's address in UK, but the next day he emailed and said that the brother of a friend of his who lived in UK was home in Albania but would be returning to England whilst I was there, and that he would happily deliver the paper to me. I thought this was all going to be too much trouble, but I was assured not. Sure enough, one day my telephone rang as I sat in my hotel room in UK and the voice at the other end of the phone introduced himself as "Vehbi", the brother of Riza's friend! He said that he had something to give me and how could we meet. I was staying in a hotel in south-west London and he lived in north-east London – for anyone unaware of travelling around London it can be a journey of a couple of uncomfortable hours driving through heavy traffic. I felt embarrassed to ask him to go to so much trouble and asked if it might be easier to meet in central London in the super Albanian "Kafe Koha", or else perhaps he could post it to me. But no, he said that he promised to put it in my hand, and that's what he was going to do, no matter how long it would take, and he would drive to my hotel that evening. He came with his wife. I tried to buy them something to eat but they said that they had eaten. Before they left, we enjoyed a drink together and talked of Shkodra, yes he was another Shkodrani! I was embarrassed at having put Vehbi and his wife to so much trouble, but part of me was so pleased to see that even living in UK some Albanians were maintaining the very best of Albanian traditions. Vehbi – you are a credit to your country.

I was sure Riza and I would meet again, and I was also sure that at least one of our more modest dreams would come to fruition. I considered him a very good friend and I hope he felt the same. I hope this essay would have given us something to chuckle about over a coffee in Shkodra. I could hardly believe the news when someone kindly contacted me to let me know he had suddenly left us.

At the time of editing this book I am at last doing a charcoal drawing of a very young Riza sitting in his MiG from that old photograph he once sent me. And I continue to search for the little children's book he wanted published in English. If only I can find it, I will do that for you my dear friend. My life is richer for having known you and you are still warming my heart and making me smile as I type this. Rest in peace my very good friend, Zoti Riza Lahi.

THE LEGEND OF ROZAFA

Travelling north from Tirana, the capital of Albania, the remains of Rozafa Castle (*Kalaja e Rozafës*), sitting atop a rocky outcrop stretching some 130 metres above the surrounding flat land, proudly and stubbornly dominating the approach to the wonderful city of Shkodra. I have mentioned this already in the first chapter, but make no excuses for repetition as it is such a glorious landmark.

As one sees the commanding views the castle has over the surrounding area it is not hard to understand why the location has always been of such strategic importance going right back in history to a time when many countries were not even discovered. It is known that this hill was the location of an Illyrian stronghold before the Romans captured it in 167 BC.

Just pause there for a second, dear reader, 167 years before Christ. 1943 years before American Independence. 2038 years before German Unification. It is staggering. Albania has such an amazingly rich and ancient history, and language, and this is a real treasure which must be maintained for future generations. In our quest for modernity and scientific advancement, and the all too common disregard for all that is considered "old", we ignore our history at our peril.

But this is not a story of philosophy and not even is it a story of Rozafa Castle, but rather more about the very person whose name this important and ancient monument has immortalized – Rozafa. As well as having such a wonderful and incredible history, and the beautiful and unique language, Albania is also the source of a plethora of folk tales, and this is one. As far as we know, Thimi Mitko (1820-1890) was the first known to record the legend in writing in his folklore collection 'Albanike melissa' (The Albanian Bee) in 1878. In this age, which some have now dubbed "Post-truth" (meaning that truth and fiction are increasingly difficult to separate, and some will tell "un-truths" deliberately to an audience which wishes to hear those very lies, and so, even though in their hearts they know them not to be true, they choose to believe them!) I will leave it up to the reader to decide how much or little of this well-known story is fact, and what is fiction.

It is said that the important task of building a castle on Mount Valdanuz was given to three well-know brothers from Shkodra. They were honoured to receive such a commission, and were in no doubt as to the importance of what they were entrusted to achieve. They set-to work with gusto, unrelentingly working every single day from dawn 'til dusk, no matter the weather or how tired they were. But every morning when they returned from their homes to the building site they discovered that whatever they had built during the previous day had somehow been demolished during the hours that they had been away. They could not understand why, and re-doubled their efforts, again and again, day after day. But still it re-occurred, every night their toil was destroyed.

After a while, in desperation, the three brothers started to look for other explanations and more importantly - solutions. It is said that a heavy fog fell over the River Buna, obscuring the flowing water for three days and three nights. Then a strong wind suddenly blew the fog away and a wise old man appeared from the dissipating mist clouds as if from nowhere. Despite the strangeness of the situation the brothers still greeted this strange apparition in the traditional manner, but recognizing that this man was no ordinary person they then poured out their frustration and confusion to him regarding the building, and how they were desperately seeking a solution. The figure looked at them with other-worldly piercing eyes and immediately and unhesitatingly told them that there was only one action to be taken. Staring steadily at each in turn, he gravely explained that the only solution was to bury one of their wives within the castle walls, and then the work could be completed unhindered.

Imagine the brothers' anxiety. They had been entrusted with this critically important work - to build a castle to protect the inhabitants of the whole city, and they worked so hard every single daylight hour of every single day, but every night their hard work was reduced to rubble. Nevertheless, the necessity to sacrifice one of their loved ones was not something which they had imagined in their wildest nightmares. They were convinced however that whatever it took to achieve their task must be done. Was this really the only option? Was this really the only solution? There must be another way! They were in no doubt as to the vitally important role the castle would play in the defences of the city they loved so dearly, but no, they were not common criminals, murderers, no! One can imagine the old man standing on that rocky hillside, looking at the three forlorn brothers and shrugging his shoulders and assuring them that this was indeed the only way to give the foundations of the castle the needed strength.

What a terrible conundrum it was for the three brothers, and the trepidation they must have felt as they struggled to find another answer. Eventually they agreed that one of their own wives must be sacrificed in order to fulfill the instructions of the mysterious visitor. To agree which one of the three it should be was impossible for the brothers. Should it be the youngest as she had been in the family for the shortest space of time, but she had her whole life in front of her. Or conversely therefore, maybe the oldest as she had already lived a decent life, at least longer than the others. But perhaps it should be the one with fewest children. It was impossible to make such a dreadful decision.

The three wives were doubtless aware of how important the building of the castle was. They must have heard their husbands discussing it day after day when they came home exhausted, and hearing how night after night their hard word was destroyed. One can envisage the wives hearing the gossip in the city, in the market and in the streets, the excitement over how the city would have a fine castle to protect them. Surely many would be praising their husbands for undertaking this demanding work, and working in such a dedicated fashion for the protection of all the citizens, but undoubtedly gossip would have also spread throughout the city about the perplexing night-time destruction and consequent lack of progress.

Each day one of the three wives would deliver lunch to the husbands, and surely they would see the frustration, confusion and exhaustion amongst the three brothers, each day repairing what had been destroyed during the previous night, working so hard, and yet with so little progress to show for their back-breaking efforts.

Unable or unwilling to make a decision regarding which of the wives should be sacrificed, the brothers agreed that whichever one of the wives delivered lunch the next day would be the chosen one, and they agreed that they would not tell their wives of the plan so that fate and fate alone would make the decision. Nevertheless, that evening when the tired men returned home the eldest brother could not bear the thought of his wife being killed, and therefore told her of the agreement and instructed her to ensure she did not deliver the next day's lunch. The middle brother also did the same, despite the promises that had been made.

Sure enough, the next day when the mother told the eldest of the three wives to deliver the lunch she lowered her eyes to the floor and replied that she was not feeling well, and couldn't go. The mother then turned to the second brother's wife and asked her to undertake the task, but she responded that she had to visit her parents. One might picture the two older wives looking everywhere but into the eyes of the mother nor the eyes of the youngest wife, knowing that they were complicit in her imminent demise. The mother then addressed the youngest wife saying, "My dear daughter-in-law, the men need bread and water and their flask of wine." The third of the women knew that the duty was hers to undertake. She could not refuse her mother-in-law and had no reason to do so except for concern that her young son would cry and need feeding. The other two daughters-in-law quietly assured her that they would look after him.

And so it was. Rozafa, the youngest wife, fetched the lunch and kissed her son goodbye and set off on the walk to Mount Valdanuz.

Visualize the scene: the three brothers hot and sweaty from the morning's work, and now here arrived the youngest of the wives. The youngest brother would undoubtedly be filled with sorrow to see his beloved slowly walking up the hill, knowing what fate awaited her. But he had made his promise and knew he must keep it. Conversely, the two older brothers would probably have been filled with mixed emotions: relief; acute embarrassment for their conniving against the younger brother; anxiety; pity; and surely most strongly they would feel shame for breaking their promise, their *besa*. As the old Albanian saying regarding *besa* expresses: *Shqiptaret vdesin dhe besen nuk e shkelin* ("Albanians would die rather than break honor"), and yet here the two oldest brothers knew that they had done just that.

I am sure that the two older brothers could not look at Rozafa eye to eye, and probably not their younger brother either. So the youngest, Rozafa's husband, was left alone to explain everything to her. Incredibly, according to the legend, Rozafa accepted her fate without argument. Her feelings of duty to her husband and for the whole community, even to sacrificing her own life in order for the castle to be completed for the protection of all the people of Shkodra, were so incredibly strong that she knew that this was her fate to fulfill. Perhaps thoughts of the other two wives' excuses that morning, and their embarrassed, furtive looks, might have flickered across her consciousness, but it was her duty as a mother that was at the forefront of her mind. Consequently, when she replied that she would accept her fate she pleaded the following:

　　*"I plead

When you place me in the wall,
Leave my right eye exposed,
Leave my right hand exposed,
Leave my right breast exposed,
Leave my right foot exposed,
For the sake of my newborn son
So that when he starts crying
Let me see him with one eye
Let me caress him with one hand
Let me feed him with one breast
Let me rock his cradle with one foot"

And then, undoubtedly with emotion, she added:

"Let my breast turn to stone and may the castle flourish.
May my son become a great hero, the ruler of the world!"

We can imagine that with those brave words Rozafa lowered her head in a gesture of surrender and readiness for self-sacrifice. The three brothers respectfully led her to the part of the wall into which she would be placed and the stones laid around her and gradually built up, leaving half of her body and face uncovered as was her wish. Her child was fetched and placed in her arms as she desired.

So it was, and sure enough as that mysterious old man had predicted, the walls remained solid and the building work continued without the hitherto mysterious nightly destruction.

However, the base of the stones around where Rozafa was entombed remained noticeably damp from the tears she was shedding for her son, and even to this very day they remain so whilst all others are dry. I have seen them such, with my own eyes.

The castle was completed and served a great purpose in defending Shkodra in many conflicts across the centuries. It was later named after Rozafa, immortalizing her for generations past, present and future. All will remember the name of Rozafa and the sacrifice she made. Who knows the names of the brothers who broke their besa, or the two older wives who had been complicit in the lie? It is Rozafa's name, and hers alone, which has been preserved. And that is as it should be.

The author's painting of Rozafa and her son.

*****

Before judging the action of the three brothers, perhaps we would do well to remember that many cultures had activities which today we would think barbaric – the Romans condemning men to death by fighting lions whilst others gleefully watched and cheered. In Spain, incredibly for a western European country in the 21st century, still people watch and cheer as bulls are mercilessly tortured to death in the most barbaric manner, excusing it as "culture"; Egyptians killing servants after the death of their master so that they could serve them in the afterlife; even into the 20th century instances of *sati* (also called *suttee)* in which Hindu widows killed themselves on their husband's funeral pyre occurred in India (even though the British had made it illegal during the days of the Raj; the Christian Crusades of the 11th- 13th centuries; let us not forget the unimaginable barbarism of Nazi German concentration camps in which hundreds of thousands were killed; or the Chinese invasion of Tibet in 1949 during which thousands of innocent Tibetans were killed, and monks were forced to have sex with nuns while the soldiers stood around laughing; and we all know all too well in our troubled times how certain (so-called) religious groups actively and deliberately murder innocent men, women and children of different faith, claiming such barbarous acts to be done in the name of God. So whilst our initial reaction to this tale may be shock that such a deed could be committed in such an ancient culture, the reality is that many atrocities are committed, even in the name of religion, to this very day, so very many centuries later.

In closing, one may draw many lessons from this tale. We can ponder on the bravery of Rozafa and her incredible self-sacrifice in order to benefit the whole community, and compare that to how many in our society today think about nothing but themselves. We can contemplate the two older brothers breaking their *besa*, and we may form our own opinion as to whether this was acceptable or not in these extreme circumstances. But we might also think about how important *besa* was in Albanian culture, and the actions of the youngest brother illustrate this, and whether or not Albanian society today (wherever it may be in the world) would benefit from remembering this, and applying it to our modern world.

Më mirë syri sesa name
Better lose your eye rather than your reputation.

KOLË IDROMENO

Kolë Idromeno is perhaps the most well-known Albanian artist of all time, and surely the father figure of art in the country, especially with regards landscape and realism. I was fortunate enough to be invited to see his most famous work, *Motra Tone*, after its return to Albania following its restoration in France.

Idromeno was born on the 15th August 1860, the same year as the famous English Impressionist artist Walter Sickert and the great Austrian composer Gustav Mahler, and in the year that Abraham Lincoln was elected as the 16th President of the United States of America. He died on the 12th December 1939, eight months after the Italian invasion of Albania at the outset of World War 2.

Kolë Idromeno is most well known as a painter, but he was also an accomplished sculptor, architect, photographer, and cinematographer. Amazingly he was also a composer and engineer during the period of history known as the Albanian Renaissance in the latter part of the nineteenth century. Almost an Albanian Leondardo Da Vinci!

He was born in Shkodra which was, of course, at that time part of the Ottoman Empire. Shkodra keeps appearing throughout this book! Shkodra had been fought over by different nationalities for centuries and was one of the main centres of culture in Albania. Some would argue it still is! His father, Arsen, was of Cham origin from Arta in what is now Greece, so let me pause on a little diversion here.

Cham Albanians (Çamë) originally came from what is now in north-west Greece, an area which Albanians call Chameria, and the Greeks call northern Epirus. The province of Epirus comprised of the four *sanjaks* of Berat, Gjirokastër, Janina and Prevesa, and Albanian was generally the spoken language, although Greek was also widely understood. They have their own particular cultural identity, naturally strongly influenced by both Greek and Albanian. They played a noteworthy role in the development of the ideas of an Albanian national identity in the latter quarter of the 19th century. To learn about the arguments, discussions, investigations and visits as to where the Greek-Albanian border should be drawn is fascinating and complex, and some would say tragic. I have touched on it again briefly in the chapter about Saranda but the history of this area deserves far more than just a few superficial sentences, so forgive me dear reader, but I must not allow myself to disappear on too much of a non-related subject, so let us return to Idromeno's father.

In 1856 Idromeno's father moved to Shkodra and remained there for the remainder of his life, working as a skilled carpenter and builder. Kolë's mother, Roza Saraçi, was a Shkodrane. How much of the unique Cham culture was passed on to Idromeno is not known, but as his father had lived most of his life in the Gheg speaking northern city of Shkodra, and Kolë was born in this city of culture, it is almost certain that the greatest influences on the young boy were from there.

A close friend of the family was the Italian artist and photographer Pjetër Marubi Born in 1834 Marubi was also a supporter of Garibaldi and for political reasons emigrated to Shkodra about 10 years before Kolë's birth. There, he founded a photographic business, *Foto Marubi*, and the Marubi National Museum of Photography remains one of the most well-known attractions of Shkodra. He gave Kolë his first lessons in photography and art. The first known works of the young boy date back to when he was just 11 years old.

Marubi recognized Idromeno's natural talent as an artist and, when Kolë reached the age of 16, Marubi encouraged and supported him to study at the prestigious Accademia di Belle Arti di Venezia. The academy was founded in 1750. The first director was the Italian Rococo painter, Giovanni Battista Piazeetta and the first president was the renowned artist Gianbattista Tiepolo, considered by some to be the best decorative artist of the 18th century. Tiepolo had died 106 years before Idromeno attended the Academy but without doubt the traditional rigours and discipline of academic art study would have remained. The Academy was at first housed in a room on the upper floor of a flour warehouse and market on the Grand Canal, close to Piazza San Marco but in 1807 it was re-founded and the name changed to the Accademia Reale di Belle Arti, and moved to premises in the more appropriate Scuola della Carita. It was here that Idromeno would have studied.

We know that he left after 6 months, but the reasons for him leaving so soon are unclear. Some have suggested that he simply disliked the formality of the art education offered by the Accademia, but at such a young age, and as the family friend Marubi had recommended and supported him, it seems surprising to me that he would have made such a bold decision alone. It may be that his course was only ever planned to be 6 months. In researching this short overview I made contact with the current Accademia who kindly checked their records, but could find no listing for Kolë Idromeno, and they could not understand why. The Accademia told me that even if a student left after 6 months his enrollment should still be listed. Could it be that he was enrolled under a different name?

Certainly in France at this time the fame of the Impressionists, with their radically un-academic methods, were very much in the public eye. The first exhibition of Impressionist art in Paris had been the publicly ridiculed Salon des Refusés in 1863, but by the time Idromeno was studying in Venice the Impressionists were gaining considerable fame. How much Kolë knew of them is not known, but it is likely that he would have heard from other artists about their revolutionary ideas regarding art.

After he left the Accademia we know that he worked in the studio of an Italian painter before traveling around parts of Europe, during which time surely he would have had much greater exposure to the Impressionists and their ideas about light and painting outdoors, with an emphasis of capturing the impression of a scene rather than an academic recording of every detail. It is also worth reminding ourselves that photography was making considerable advances by the 1870s, and many saw this as replacing paint on canvas, thus increasing the belief amongst some artists that the work of the painter must depict something more than that which a photographic image could record. Painting, they argued, should be about emotion and impression, and no longer the need for an ultra-accurate, slavish record of every precise detail – that was the camera's job, they argued. I would suggest that such ideas must surely have excited and influenced the maturing Kolë to some extent.

By the time he was 18, in 1878, Idromeno decided to return to his beloved Shkodra. Undoubtedly bursting with excitement over all that he must have seen during his travels he threw himself into a wide variety of different endeavours: painting, sculpture, photography, music composure, and even some engineering projects. He opened a photographic studio called "Dritëshkronja Idromeno".

At that very same time there was a growing strengthening of nationalist feeling in the country. The year that he returned, 1878, was an extremely important year in Albanian history as it was the year that the Prizren League ("League for the Defense of the Rights of the Albanian Nation") was officially established. The famous Albanian Pashko Vasa wrote his famous poem "O Moj Shqypni" sometime between 1878 and 1880 (see next section of this book) urging all Albanians to national awakening and unity, transcending religious and other identities which he believed were keeping the Albanians divided. Fired up by youth and patriotism and the intellectual group to which he belonged, the young Idromeno became a strong advocate for the independence of Albania from the Ottoman Empire, and his publicly expressed stance later led to his exile to Ulcinj in Montenegro, 42 kilometres from his beloved Shkodra.

Until 1896, Idromeno painted mainly paintings with religious themes which, after the exposure he must have received during his travels in Europe, may be surprising, but probably this was what the market demanded in Shkodra at that time. Afterwards, however, he painted scenes of everyday life and realistic portraits and it is with these that he is most well remembered. Buildings, costumes and contemporary life were recorded accurately in these wonderful works which remain an accurate source of reference to this day. Their artistic merits are considerable with skillful use of colour and composition, demonstrating Idromeno's true talent.

Probably his most famous work is "Motra Tone" ("Sister Tona") which he painted in 1883, and which some have called the Mona Lisa of Albania. It was this beautiful painting of his sister, Tona, which was my first introduction to Idromeno. According to the researcher Mikel Prenushi ("Kol Idromeno" monograph, life and work, "8 Nëntori", 1984) Idromeno started the painting in early January 1883, and his sister posed for him in traditional Shkodrane costume for 7 - 8 days. He then finished the painting shortly thereafter and signed it on 2nd February 1883. Influences of the Italian Renaissance period can be seen in the painting. The pose is especially unusual and intriguing as Tona looks out to the side of the picture, seemingly avoiding eye contact with the viewer, and with one hand partly covering her face with her white veil one might deduce an attitude of shyness. Is it too much of a stretch of the imagination to suggest similarities with the enigmatic smile of the Mona Lisa? Perhaps, and yet as with Mona Lisa, I find myself pondering the manner in which viewers see and understand Tona in different ways from the painting. Speaking personally, I never tire looking at this painting. Surely these two aspects, are signs of a true masterpiece! As I look deeper into the painting I see a strength and confidence in the young lady, despite the apparent shyness of her pose. The folds and curves of the white veil are expertly painted as are the hands, which Idromeno has captured beautifully.

It is believed that the masterpiece was given to his sister, but sadly she died seven years later. Idromeno then kept the portrait in his studio as a reminder of his beloved sister. After his death the painting remained within Idromeno's family until being exhibited publicly for the first time in 1954. It was restored by the Musee de France and exhibited in the Musee D'Orsay in 2005 before being returned to Albanian where it is now, quite rightly, one of the star attractions of the National Art Gallery of Albania.

Other examples of his most important paintings depicted the scenes of everyday life. One of my own favourites, and another very well know painting, is his wonderful 1924 painting *"Dasma shkodrane"* ("Wedding in Shkodra") in which he accurately recorded the dress of the men and women of the wedding party, set within the background of typical Shkodra buildings. The expressions of the different figures are very skillfully painted. His use of rich colour set against whites and earth tones is sublime, and the different textures and clever composition truly make this one of his greatest masterpieces.

In 1923 he organised an art exhibition in Shkodra, which it is believed was the very first such exhibition in the city. Unsurprisingly he was represented in the first national art exhibition in Tirana in 1931. His own works have been shown at various international art exhibitions, including in Budapest (1898), Rome (1925), Bari (1931), Rome (1936) and New York (1939).

So, what of his other talents? Well, Idromeno first showed motion pictures at the Gjuha Shqipe Cultural Centre in 1908 and 4 years later, in August 1912, having signed some form of contract with the Austrian company Josef Stauber to establish Albania's first public cinema, was the first cinematographer to show foreign motion pictures in Albania.

As an architect, he designed over 60 buildings, private, public and industrial. These included the "Vila e Shirokës" (1925–26), "Centrali elektrik" (1928), "Banka e Shtetit"(1930), "Kinemaja Rozafat"(1935), and the "Kafja e madhe" (1935).

The coffered ceiling of the St. Stephen's Cathedral (Kisha e Madhe) in Shkodra was also his design. The 74 metre long, 50 metre wide, 23½ metre tall cathedral, initially with standing room for 6,000 worshippers, is one of the largest in the Balkans. Permission had been granted to build the Cathedral in 1851 but it was not until 1909 that Idromeno coffered the vault. A coffered ceiling comprises of a series of sunken panels used as decoration, the strength of the structure is in the framework of the coffers. Some of Idromeno's paintings may be seen in the Cathedral and one of particular interest is the "Lady of Shkoder" which has angels dressed in typical Shkodra folk costumes with the city clearly seen in the background.

In the General Directorate of Archives of Albania (Drejtorinë e Përgjithëshme të Arkivave të Shqipërisë) the drawings of the picture "Shkodra Wedding" are preserved. A collection of his photographic negatives is retained in the archive of the Qëndrës Albanologjike, Tiranë, (Albanian Center of Albanology, Tirana).

Truly the Renaissance man, with interests in so many burgeoning fields, his paintings remain his most well-known legacy, although with the buildings he designed, the appearance of parts of Shkodra would not be the same today if not for him. His contribution to the photographic records of Shkodran life are second only to those of Marubi, and after all, as it was Marubi who encouraged and supported the young Idromeno to study art in Venice, so perhaps that is the correct order of things!

The name of Idromeno is known to all Shkodrans, and the main pedestrianized street, and arguably the most beautiful, is named after him, Rruga Kolë Idromeno, and that is exactly as it should be.

O MOJ SHQYPNI

Here is the famous poem by Pashko Vasa, written sometime betwen 1878-80, which was about the time Idromeno returned to Shkodra. (Translation appears under the Albanian.)

O MOJ SHQYPNI

O moj Shqypni, e mjera Shqypni,
Kush te ka qitë me krye n'hi?
Ti ke pas kenë një zojë e randë,
Burrat e dheut të thirrshin nanë.
Ke pasë shumë t'mira e begati,
Me varza t'bukura e me djelm t'ri,
Gja e vend shumë, ara e bashtina,
Me armë të bardha, me pushkë ltina,
Me burra trima, me gra të dlira;
Ti ndër gjith shoqet ke kenë ma e mira.
Kur kriste pushka si me shkrep moti,
Zogu i shqyptarit gjithmonë i zoti
Ka kenë për luftë e n'luftë ka dekun
E dhunë mbrapa kurr s'i mbetun.
Kur ka lidhë besën burri i Shqypnisë,
I ka shti dridhën gjithë Rumelisë;
Ndër lufta t'rrebta gjithëkund ka ra,
Me faqe t'bardhë gjithmonë asht da.

Por sot, Shqypni, pa m'thuej si je?
Po sikur lisi i rrxuem përdhe,
Shkon bota sipri, me kambë, të shklet
E nji fjalë t'ambël askush s'ta flet.
Si mal me borë, si fushë me lule
Ke pas qenë veshun, sot je me crule,
E s'të ka mbetun as em'n as besë;
Vet e ke prishun për faqe t'zezë.
Shqyptar', me vllazën jeni tuj u vra,
Ndër nji qind ceta jeni shpërnda;
Ca thone kam fè ca thonë kam din;
Njeni:"jam turk", tjetri:"latin"
Do thonë: "Jam grek", "shkje"-disa tjerë,
Por jemi vllazën t'gjith more t'mjerë!
Priftnit e hoxhët ju kanë hutue,

Për me ju damun me ju vorfnue!
Vjen njeri i huej e ju rri n'votër,
Me ju turpnue me grue e motër,
E për sa pare qi do t'fitoni,
Besën e t'parëve t'gjith e harroni,
Baheni robt e njerit t'huej,
Qi nuk ka gjuhën dhe gjakun tuej.
Qani ju shpata e ju dyfeqe,
Shqiptari u zu si zog ndër leqe!
Qani ju trima bashkë me ne,
Se ra Shqypnia me faqe n'dhe!
E s'i ka mbetun as bukë as mish,
As zjarm në votër, as dritë, as pishë;
As gjak në faqe, as nder ndër shokë,
Por asht rrëxue e bamun trokë!
Mblidhniu ju varza, mblidhniu ju gra,
M'ata sy t'bukur q'dini me qa,
Eni t'vajtojmë Shqypninë e mjerë,
Qi mbet' e shkretë pa em'n, pa nder;
Ka mbet e vejë si grue pa burrë,
Ka mbet si nanë, qi s'pat djalë kurrë!
Kujt i ban zemra m'e e lan' me dekë
Kët farë trimneshe, qi sot asht mekë?
Këtë nanë të dashtun a do ta lamë,
Qi njeri i huej ta shklasë me kambë?
Nuk, nuk! Këtë marrè askush s'e do
Këtë faqe t'zezë gjithkush e dro!
Para se t'hupet kështu Shqypnia,
Me pushkë n'dorë le t'desë trimnia!
Coniu, shqyptarë, prej gjumit çoniu,
Të gjithë si vllazën n'nji besë shtërngoniu,
E mos shikoni kisha e xhamia:
Feja e shqyptarit asht shqyptaria!
Qysh prej Tivarit deri n'Prevezë,
Gjithkund lshon dielli vap'edhe rrezë,
Asht tok' e jona, prind na e kanë lanë
Kush mos na e preki, se desim t'tanë

Të desim si burrat që vdiqnë motit
Edhe mos marrohna përpara zotit.

Oh Albania, Poor Albania

Oh Albania, poor Albania,
Who has shoved your head in ashes?
Once you were a fine, great lady,
All the world's men called you mother.
Once you had such wealth and goodness,
With fair maidens, strapping young lads,
Herds and land, rich fields and produce,
Flashing guns, Italian weapons,
Heroic fellows and pure women,
You reigned as their best companion.

At rifle's blast, at flash of lightning
The Albanian mastered battle,
Thus he fought and thus he perished,
Leaving ne'er misdeeds behind him.
Whene'er an Albanian swore an oath did
All the Balkans tremble at him,
When he charged in savage battle,
Always he returned a victor.

How fare you today, Albania?
Like an oak tree groundward falling!
Trampled now, the world walks o'er you,
No one has a kind word for you.
Like snow-capped peaks, like fields a-blooming
You were clothed, you're now in tatters,
You've no name or reputation,
In your plight you have destroyed them.

Albanians, you are killing kinfolk,
You're split in a hundred factions,
Some believe in God or Allah,

Say 'I'm Turk,' or 'I am Latin,'
Say 'I'm Greek,' or 'I am Slavic,'
But you're brothers, hapless people!
You've been duped by priests and hodjas
To divide you, keep you wretched,
When the stranger shares your hearth side,
Puts to shame your wife and sister,
You still serve him, gaining little,
You forget your forebears' pledges
You are serfs to foreign landlords,
Who have not your blood or language!
Weep, lament, oh swords and rifles,
The Albanian bird's been snared, imprisoned!
Weep with us, oh dauntless heroes,
For Albania's toppled, face-smeared,
Neither bread nor meat remaining,
Fire in hearth, nor light, nor pine torch,
Drained of blood and of friends' honour,
She's defiled and now has fallen!

Gather 'round now, maids and women,
You with fair eyes know of weeping,
Come and mourn our poor Albania,
She has lost her honour, virtue,
She's a widow with no husband,
She's a mother with no offspring!

Who has the heart to let her perish,
Once a heroine, now so weakened!
Well-loved mother, dare we leave her
To fall under foreign boot heels?

No one wishes such shame on her,
Each of us dreads such misfortune!
Before Albania's thus forsaken
Let our men die, bearing rifles.

Wake, Albanian, from your slumber,
Let us, brothers, swear in common
And not look to church or mosque,
The Albanian's faith is Albanianism!

From Bar down to far Preveza
Shall the sun spread forth its warm rays,
Our forefathers left us this land,
Let none touch it, for we'll all die!
Let us fall as did our forebears
And not shame ourselves before God!

[Translated by Robert Elsie.]

(See Annex B for "A Selection of Books by Robert Elsie in the English Language")

URA E MESIT
THE MES BRIDGE – NEAR SHKODRA

During my month in Shkodra, Justina offered to take me to see the famous Ura e Mesit, one of the most important Ottoman bridges in Albania, located in the village of Mes, just over 9 kilometres from the city. It was built between 1768 and 1770 by Kara Mahmud Bushati, more about him later. This important bridge spans the river Kir which flows roughly southwest down from the Northern Albanian Alps until it joins the river Drin just outside the city.

We travelled north-east, past the hospital and the old industrial area, and I noted a few small signposts, which seemed far too modest for such an important historical structure. The bridge, linking Shkodra with the village of Drisht, and from there up into Kosovo, played an important role for Shkodra which was a hub for trade and communication through the centuries.

I learnt that Drisht (Drivastum) is 6 kilometres from the bridge and has a rich history itself. The village, a former bishopric, has the remains of a castle (*Kalaja e Drishtit*) which dates back to the 13th century, but whose history extends considerably earlier than that. It is known that as early as the 9th century, maybe earlier, the fortifications once formed part of the defences of the Zeta Principality. The Principality of Zeta (now in Montenegro) was a medieval state based around Lake Shkodra until the Ottoman conquest in 1498 when it fell during the Siege of Shkodra. Above the village today are archaeological remains of late-Roman and medieval Drivastum. I made a mental note that one day I must visit this, yet another fascinating area of ancient Albanian history.

As I looked at the amazing Ura e Mesit, 108 metres long, 3.4 meters, wide and 12½ meters high, I was unsurprised that it is listed as one of the longest and finest Ottoman bridges in the Balkans.

I imagined how many incredible stories could be told about who had crossed the 13 arches of the bridge, and I was awe-inspired by the beautiful mountainous backdrop. But yes, I must admit that my heart wept a silent tear when the all too apparent, and all too frequently seen, rubbish surrounding the bridge suggested a lack of care or acknowledgment of what treasures the Albanian people have. Such an amazing history and yet so much of its physical evidence could all too easily be swept away in a single unthinking, uncaring generation. I can only hope that times have changed since I first saw the bridge – some have told me that there have been considerable improvements and I hope to visit again soon in order to see for myself.

Very noticeable is that the bridge does not follow a straight-line but has a 14-degree bend about 5 metres from the central arch. As an artist, I smiled and thought that some day I would like to paint it, but that anyone unfamiliar with this kink in the structure would think that I was drunk when they saw my depiction on canvas!

Ura e Mesit.

The construction of the Ura e Mesit was in two phases. I should say here that I have read two differing accounts, but the one I favour is that the middle arch and two arches on one side and one on the other side of the centre was the first phase, and the second phase of building completed the bridge as we see it today. The builder, Kara Mahmud Bushati (1749-1796), was a hereditary Ottoman governor (a mutasarrif) of the sanjak of Shkoder - a "sanjak" being an administrative region and subdivision of a "vilayet" under the Ottoman Empire. The Bushatis were an old Albanian family. Mahmud's father, Mehmed (or Mehmet) Bushati, had been the governor of the sanjak of Scutari and is known to have built the famous Leaden Mosque near Rozafa Castle in 1773. When he died, two years later, the governorship was passed to Mahmud. According to Miranda Vickers in her excellent book "The Albanians, a Modern History" it was under Kara Mahmud that the Pashalik (the jurisdiction or area of control of a Pasha, or regional governor) of Shkoder achieved distinction with Mahmud behaving more

130

like an independent prince, extending his rule north into Kosovo and south as far as Berat.

As an aside, Miranda Vickers is not a relative of mine, despite the shared family name (which is not so common, and so makes the coincidence even greater, and even more so as her ancestors came from the same city as my father's). We exchanged a few emails years ago, and once met for coffee when she was visiting Tirana. Anyhow, back to the story........

Mahmud refused to blindly kowtow to the Ottoman rulers and it is believed that in the 1780s things came to a head because of his expressed desire to create an independent principality. One may often read that in 1785 he attacked Montenegro, setting fire to Cetinje and destroying the monastery, and whilst this is true, we should also remember that Cetinje was also a sanctuary for the many pirates of the area at that time, and it was their destruction which was his goal, and in which he succeeded. Mahmud also had a conflict with the Tosk Pashas of southern Albania, especially with the famous, if now controversial, Ali Pasha.

The Austrians and Russians sent a delegation to offer him support to fight against the Turks, with the stated aim of him converting to Christianity and becoming King of the Albanian-speaking people. Initially he accepted their proposal, but then in 1788 he discovered that the Austrians and Russians had the hidden agenda to cede his area of northern Albania to Montenegro. He promptly beheaded the delegation and sent their heads to the Ottoman Sultan who, in return, pardoned him for his past actions. This was not the first time, and wouldn't be the last, that the so-called Great Powers attempted to use Albanians as pawns in their game for dominance of the area.

Still Mahmud chose not to live quietly and annexed the sanjak of Prizren and large parts of Montenegro. He also carried out military and political reforms in the areas under his control, but without the required agreement from the Ottoman rulers. The Turks' response was to send a military force to besiege Shkodra.

After some time the siege was lifted and the Ottoman expedition retreated, only to return once more, but failing to achieve their aim.

Kara Mahmud Pasha launched another offensive against Montenegro in 1796 that eventually led to his defeat and indeed his decapitation. His skull gruesomely continues to be displayed in the orthodox monastery at Cetinje.

Such is the history which Ura e Mesit can tell.

Bronze Age burial items have been found in the vicinity of the bridge.

Subsequent to my time in Albania I understand that the Albanian Development Fund invested 13 million lekë to undertake restorative work for the bridge, and it is now a well-established tourist attraction for anyone visiting northwest Albania. Ura e Mesit continues to create new traditions and it is now a popular spot for newly married couples to visit for photographs, and some say that they receive blessings from the bridge for their future happiness. Perhaps it is not the bridge itself but the hundreds and hundreds of years of colourful characters who have been connected with the bridge and who have imbibed it with their positive energy and the life force of Albanian tradition and history!

As we left Ura e Mesit to return to Shkodra my mind was abuzz with all that I had heard and read about the history connected to the bridge. As I hope this tale has briefly recounted, it is not simply "a bridge" but rather, if one pauses to look deeper, it has so much to tell us about the history of the time and area, and the people and places connected to it. And it is so wonderful that even today it is creating new histories, attracting more and more people, all of whom will have their own little piece of history connected to Ura e Mesit. Long may it continue, and may it be treasured for the real gem it is. History is not dead but something alive and growing with us every day and as I have said elsewhere, what we do today is tomorrow's history.

When I left the wonderful hospitality of Domenika and Justina after a month staying in their lovely home and feeling that I had a new adopted family, I was left speechless when they gave me the most wonderful present – a beautiful oil painting of Ura e Mesit by the artist Liljana Çefa. The painting has been a treasure in my home ever since, first in Tirana, then in Kathmandu, and now in Taiwan. As for my own artistic endeavours, I have now started a small painting of this iconic landmark and hope it will provide a catalyst for telling many more people about the rich history of Albania.

THE BRITISH IN ALBANIA
DURING WORLD WAR TWO

When I lived in Albania I had an aspiration to write a book about the British servicemen who died there during World War Two. The idea was to describe the lives of these young men rather than detailed accounts of their operations – that has been written about in detail by others. I wanted to learn about who those men were as individuals. Why did they volunteer for these amazingly dangerous duties, which led some to lose their lives in this small Balkan country, a country which I had come to love so dearly? What was their motivation? And what of the conflicting opinions I so frequently heard from Albanians and foreigners regarding who did what, and who didn't?

Part of me feels that it is something of an indulgence for me to include this chapter when I am so very aware of how many more Albanians showed immense bravery during the Second World War compared to a few dozen British servicemen, and many Albanians lost their lives fighting for freedom during the war and in the years thereafter. I have decided to include it however as I also wanted to attempt to add some balance to the last sentence of the previous paragraph – the conflicting opinions – and it is also provides me with an excuse to summarise the situation in the country at that time. It was such a critical period which affected several generations to come. So for my Albanian friends, please take this chapter in the spirit in which it is mean and the perspective expressed in this paragraph.

I will provide a list of British casualties, but will consign that to an annex.

The British have a memorial park in Tirana with 46 memorial stones. Sadly, this is not the actual location where those brave men were actually buried. During the grim days of Hoxha's communism the bodies were dug up from their original burial sites and thrown into a mass grave. This is now unmarked, under a path somewhere behind the university buildings in Tirana, close to what is now the Memorial Park. I tried to locate the exact spot and whilst I managed to match ground-signs of the location with period photographs, no one seemed able, or willing, to categorically confirm this. Maybe it just didn't seem important to anyone else but me, or perhaps there was concern about what I might then wish to do, or could it just have been embarrassment about what had been done.

Here is the entry on the British Commonwealth War Graves Commission website:

> *Following the end of the war in Europe, an Army Graves Registration Unit entered Albania with the task of concentrating the remains of Commonwealth Servicemen, lost in the struggle to secure Albania freedom, into a site chosen in the capital, Tirana. However, due to the political situation in the country, this task could not be completed, though 52 sets of remains were recovered in the short time available. Eventually, in 1955, after repeated requests to enter the country were refused, the Commission took the decision to commemorate the 38 identified casualties on special memorials erected in Phaleron War Cemetery in Greece. This situation remained thus until 1994, when a change in the political situation in Albania allowed a Commission representative access for the first time. He discovered that the original individual burials had been moved by the Communist authorities to an unmarked collective grave located under a path near the university buildings in Tirana. At the beginning of 1995, the 38 special memorials were removed from Phaleron and re-erected as close as possible to the site of the mass grave, in an area designated the Tirana Park Memorial Cemetery. In 1998, following a study of the Graves Registration unit files, it was possible for the Commission's records staff to confirm the identities of a further seven casualties previously buried in Tirana War Cemetery as unknowns.*

The author paying his respects in the British Memorial Park.

Regrettably time for detailed research was limited whilst I was in Albania as I dedicated myself heart and soul to my busy job. The idea to write a book therefore fell into the "at some future time" category. Nevertheless, I contacted the various regimental associations asking for any information they might have on the names for which I had but the scantiest of details, but sadly I received few replies. Initially I was bitterly disappointed. I had to face facts however - whilst for me this *was* important, for the military museums and various archives back in UK these were such small-scale military operations in comparison to other campaigns where hundreds and thousands of British men had fought and lost their lives. I was attempting to research the lives of 46 men coming from multiple different military units, whereas by the end of the War, UK would have suffered 383,700 military casualties and 67,200 civilian deaths due to military activities, in addition to the million British men who had lost their lives in the First World War (1914-18) less than 25 years earlier.

It may be worthy to note in the context of this account that taken as a percentage of the overall population of the country, UK casualties in World War Two were less than half those suffered by Albania.

THE WIDER BRITISH WAR EFFORT

It is necessary to put the British war effort in Albania into a wider perspective before judging what some may too assess to be far from a glorious chapter in British military history, and indeed some may even see as betrayal or shameful. I make no excuse for the length of this introduction as only with such perspective may one fairly understand UK's involvement in Albania.

From September 1939 until late 1941, Britain led Allied efforts in almost every global military theatre. Nearly 15 million men and women from UK and her Commonwealth fought the German, Italian, Japanese and other Axis armies, air forces and navies across the world in a mammoth effort to slow or stop the Axis advance.

From early summer of 1940, following the German steamroller invasions of Poland, Denmark, Norway, France, Belgium, Luxembourg and the Netherlands, the British and Commonwealth was standing almost alone against Germany and her allies until the USSR entered the war in June 1941. The Americans didn't enter the war until December 1941 by which time the British had been fighting for over two years.

The UK mainland had also come under large-scale attack. The German air force, the Luftwaffe, attacked England between July and October 1940 in what became known as the Battle of Britain. UK and her Commonwealth had 1,542 aircrew killed, 422 wounded and 1,744 aircraft destroyed. The Germans attacked not only military targets but bombed London and other cities also, and an estimated 90,000 civilian casualties resulted, 40,000 of them fatal. To Hitler's immense frustration the Royal Air Force bravely and stoically continued to fight in the skies over England, despite numerical inferiority and the considerable losses, and succeeded in defeating the Luftwaffe to such an extent that they were never to fully recover. The Luftwaffe lost 2,585 aircrew killed or missing, 925 captured, 735 wounded and 1,977 aircraft destroyed.

UK was also hosting numerous governments in exile back in London and the diplomatic effort (and in some cases financial support) must have been exceptionally complex.

Considering all this, the British attitude in Albania during World War Two becomes more understandable.

THE SITUATION IN ALBANIA

Conversely, one must also attempt to understand the situation from an Albanian perspective. The situation in Albania had become complicated after the Italian invasion and the exile of King Zog. Three active opposition groups formed: the Legaliteti (*Lëvizja Legalitetit*) translated as the Legality Movement) who were nationalists who supported King Zog was founded in 1941; the National   Liberation   Movement (*Lëvizja   Nacional-Çlirimtare* or *Lëvizja Antifashiste Nacional-Çlirimtare (LANÇ)*), also translated as *National Liberation Front*, and often simply called the Partisans (many of whom were communist, but at least earlier on it may be argued that many were not) was officially created in September 1942; and the Balli Kombëtar (literally *National Front*), known as Balli, who were strongly anti-communist nationalists, but did not support King Zog was founded in December 1942.

In Blendi Fevziu's excellent biography of the post-War communist dictator of Albania, *"Enver Hoxha, The Iron Fist of Albania"* he states:

> *"Documents that have come to light recently have revealed that Hoxha was convinced that an Allied victory was just a matter of time, he focussed his efforts on strengthening his position as leader and removing any impediments to his post-war rise to power."*

He also writes:

> *"The advice he [Hoxha] had been given by the Yugoslavs…. was to avoid publicly referring to the CPA [Communist Party of Albania] as the leader of the Albanian resistance movement. Instead, Hoxha would usually speak of a 'patriotic resistance movement', in which the communists had a role to play, albeit not a central one."*

So, it is indeed possible that some who sided with the Partisans were not committed communists, at least in the early period, and did not understand the strategic longer-term aims of Hoxha. And once they did realise, if they spoke out, it was fatal.

The British Government could, and arguably should, have shown more public support for King Zog who settled in UK in exile. In not doing so they must surely not have helped his cause as the rightful ruler of Albania, nor those who supported him and who could have been instrumental in the fight against the invaders – Italy, and subsequently Germany. I have read numerous reports regarding UK's attitude to King Zog, and it amazes me how polarized opinions were. Some dismissed him outright, whilst others (and often these seem to be those British men who had personally known him in Albania) supported him most strongly, spoke up on his behalf at every opportunity, and petitioned the British government in the most strident of manners.

A photograph from the author's collection:
"Shtyllë: British officers and members of Albanian shtab. *Left to right: Dali Ndreu, Andy Hands, Ramadan Çitaku, Spiro Moisi, Billy McLean, Garry Duffy, Enver Hoxha, Tony Neel.*

UK was a strong supporter of Greece, Albania's southern neighbour, which had territorial ambitions to take over a large part of the south of the country, as I have briefly mentioned in a previous chapter. According to reports, they greatly influenced London not to support King Zog because they saw him to be an obstacle to their own territorial claims. Some evidence suggests that the Yugoslavs also exerted pressure, with their own desires on Albanian territory in the north. London bowed to the pressure in the game of diplomacy and power-play, and consequently did not officially recognise the King's government-in-exile. Official papers from this period have only recently been released in UK, and some time and care needs to be taken in piecing together all this evidence regarding the British attitude before accurate conclusions can be reached as, from what I have seen, attitudes changed over time, and some evidence seems contradictory. It would be too easy to take one piece of evidence out of context and reach a totally erroneous conclusion.

The Italians invaded Albania in 1939, two days after the birth of King Zog's son, Leka I, and the King had little option but, like many other national monarchs and leaders, to go into exile, arriving in London sometime thereafter. In 1943 the Germans replaced the Italians as the occupying force.

THE FIRST BRITISH ATTEMPTS

The first British involvement was in 1941 when Major Oakley-Hill, a former adviser to the Albanian Gendarmerie, led approximately 200 (some accounts say 300) Albanian exiles across the border from Yugoslavia. It was a mission doomed to failure however, quickly coming under attack. Many of the Albanians successfully disappeared into the hills, whilst Oakley-Hill and others captured. The British Major spent the next 2½ years as a prisoner of war.

THE BRITISH TRY AGAIN

It wasn't until the Spring of 1943 that the British tried again with the insertion of Major Neil "Billy" McLean and David Smiley and this phase continued until October of that year when Brigadier "Trotsky" Davies' entered Albania. The British plans were to insert small groups of highly trained and motivated men into the country with the aim of linking up with any of the factions prepared to fight the Germans.

Until what some have designated the fourth stage, from April 1944 until the end of the war in 1945, some may argue that the British had not fully understood the true nature of the Partisans, but this, and especially the ambitions of their leader, Enver Hoxha, were becoming all too clear after Hoxha ordered that any of the British who were helping any non-Partisan groups should be captured, tortured or killed.

Photograph from the author's collection:
"Bixha: Smiley, Fred Nosi and Baba Faja signing for weapons.

THE BRITISH VIEWPOINT

As I hope is therefore clear from my very lengthy introduction, from a purely British point of view, their aim was not to get involved in internal Albanian politics, but rather to encourage and support any Albanian group which was prepared to fight the Germans, full-stop. They hoped to divert German resources and attention, cause whatever damage they could, but without tying down already very stretched British resources.

However, reading some of the autobiographies of British officers who were involved, some gave repeated warnings to their hierarchy about the dangerous nature of the Partisans and what they could predict might be the aftermath. Sadly, their warnings were ignored and it would seem that some messages never left the SOE headquarters in Bari, or arrived in London far too late for them to be of value. To this day there are accusations that some within the SOE organization, especially perhaps in Bari, were strongly left-wing biased and therefore unblinkingly supported the Partisans in full knowledge of the consequences. This is a matter of argument.

THE ALBANIAN VIEWPOINT

If we look from a purely Albanian perspective however, the brave Albanians who *were* prepared to fight a massively superior invader, faced dire consequences for themselves and their whole communities if caught. They were fighting for national survival, not passing visitors who could (if they survived) return home once the war was over. The Albanians would have to live with the resulting situation. The viewpoint is consequently very different.

Add to this the growing realisation amongst Ballists and Zogists, which proved to be absolutely correct, that the Partisans had a much more sinister longer term aim of not only ridding the country of its invaders, but also to seize total control after the war was over, and possibly forming some sort of Balkan communist federation. The reluctance of the British to give more support than they did, and worse – to see the British donating considerable amounts of weapons, ammunition and gold to the communist Partisans must have seemed like a complete betrayal.

NOT ONLY IN ALBANIA

It is noteworthy, and perhaps some similarities to the situation in Albania can be drawn, that after the Japanese invasion of Malaya in 1941 the Malayan Communist Party (MCP) established an underground movement, and the British gave intense training to 200 of the MCP guerillas and helped them establish camps deep in the jungle. This developed into the 7,000 strong Malayan People's Anti-Japanese Army. The British believed that the guerillas, properly trained, armed and coordinated, could be useful in the planned invasion to recapture Malaya. Officers from "Force 136" were parachuted into the jungle areas from 1943 onwards and were, seemingly, welcomed, protected, fed and looked after by the MCP. In return the British supplied the guerillas with weapons, ammunition and other supplies. However, as soon as it became clear that the Japanese were losing the war, the communists started to stockpile the British weapons and ammunition which had been supplied specifically to fight the Japanese, in preparation for the end of the war and the subsequent overthrow of the British and the establishment of a communist state. The British "Force 136" officers realized the dangers of the situation and attempted to disband the guerilla groups, trying to entice the individuals to surrender their weapons with medals and cash, but this was only partially successful and large quantities of ammunition and weapons remained unaccounted for. These were then used against the British in the "Malayan Emergency" between 1948 – 1960.

NO COORDINATION BETWEEN FACTIONS

Returning to Albania, it was increasingly clear that there would be no consensus or agreement between the various factions to fight the Germans in any consolidated fashion. Clearly some local leaders seemed keener to persuade the British to supply them with weapons and ammunition not to use against the Germans but to stash away for use in the civil war against communism which seemed increasingly inevitable. At the same time, the Partisans were also using British supplied weapons and ammunition to kill fellow Albanians who had any disagreement with them, and later also for political positioning within their own group. Later, as briefly mentioned already, the weapons supplied by London were also used against the British military. One can imagine the frustration of those brave British men, some of whom had parachuted into the country alone and were doing whatever they could to urge the different groups to fight, and preferably to fight together against a common enemy.

Looking at it from an Albanian perspective, I am sure that some would have felt equally frustrated at the British strategic decisions which were being made, especially as they witnessed the cold-blooded attitude of the Partisans against the other Albanian groups which the British were (at least initially) working alongside. One can understand from an Albanian perspective that a post-war communist dictatorship was a much more dangerous threat than that posed by the Germans, and tragically they were proved correct.

Photograph from the author's collection:
Corporal "Cuni" Davis and his wireless set.

There were attempts to persuade the various groups to fight together both from Albanian initiatives and from the British, but all came to naught. One attempt was the *"Mukja Agreement"* of August 1943 when delegations from the National Liberation Council and Balli Kombetar signed an agreement which should have established a *"Joint Committee for the Salvation of Albania"*. A few days later however Enver Hoxha sent out a letter to all Communist party chapters repudiating the *"Mukja Agreement"* and instead attacked the Ballists. It is thought that Hoxha's action was undertaken partly with pressure, or at least influence, from the Montenegrin Miladin Popovic who was concerned at the prospect of an "ethnic Albania" which would include Kosovo. A form of "neutral words" had been agreed at Mukja in an attempt to reach compromise over this sticking point. The Ballists emphasised the creation of an ethnic Albania and Albanian independence, whereas the communists, at that time, and with Yugoslav influence, wished for a "federation of Balkan countries".

ABAZ KUPI

Another of the efforts to collaborate was with Abaz Kupi, sometimes known under the nickname "Bazi i Canes". Kupi had been a commander in King Zog's gendarmerie and resisted the 1939 Italian invasion in Durres as strongly as was possible. He then fled to Yugoslavia and later met up with the British officer Julian Amery who encouraged him to re-enter Albania to fight the occupiers. This he did in 1941 with 300 fighters. At the Peza Conference he was elected deputy chairman of the National Liberation Council and fought alongside the Partisans until 1943. When Hoxha reneged on the *Mukja Agreement* and issued a ban on King Zog from returning to Albania, Kupi decided to lead the *Legaliteti* party. His basic premise was that King Zog was the only one with a legitimate claim to govern the country. A British mission was attached to his headquarters.

By mid-1944 Kupi was under no illusions concerning the real aim of the communists – post-war rule of the country, and Hoxha knew that Kupi was the greatest threat to his future takeover of the country. The well organised and numerically superior Partisans moved north and attacked Kupi's men. The most fatal blow to Kupi however came from the British when the SOE headquarters in Bari, desperate to keep Hoxha's men fighting the Germans, ordered support to Kupi to cease. There is some evidence that this was a demand made by Hoxha to the British. The British who had been attached to Kupi's groups were ordered to evacuate, and in what many saw as a complete betrayal, there was a specific order that Kupi could not be evacuated with them. Nevertheless, and returning to my theme of looking at the individuals on the ground, away from the nameless and faceless cold politics, Amery argued vehemently for support for Kupi, refusing to desert him, and eventually raising the issue up to Churchill personally. Such was the strength of the plea that fresh orders were issued which included the evacuation of Kupi from his inevitable fate at the hands of the communists, but by that time he had already left Albania. As a final note, Kupi spent his last years living in New York, always under threat from the Albanian Sigurimi (secret services), and died in 1976, aged 84. Thousands attended his funeral, and I feel of particular note to this record - the ceremony was led by his old comrade in arms, Julian Amery. Surely this further and irrefutable evidence that, away from the frustrations of politics and strategic policy, at least amongst some of those brave British and Albanian men on the ground, exceptionally strong bonds of lifelong friendship and respect were forged, never to be broken.

PARTISAN STRENGTH

It seems that one reason why the Partisans were gaining such a foothold and achieving greater success than the Ballists and Zogists was because their command structure was more effective.

Regrettably, far too frequently, the various anti-communist clan leaders did not coordinate their efforts and were reluctant to accept any central leadership.

GERMAN PROMISES

It is also worth noting that the Germans were making assurances about Kosovo being returned to Albania after the war, and also guaranteeing Albanian independence, whereas the British only talked of fighting the Germans and would make no such guarantees, saying that it would all be decided *after* the War.

Whether or not the German promises would have been kept is another issue altogether – it certainly would not be the first time that false promises had deliberately been made to Albania by one of the more powerful nations, but nevertheless it may be hardly surprising that at least some Albanians sympathised more with the Germans than with the Allies. Or if not actively supporting the Germans, at least thinking that the Albanian partisans were a greater threat to the future of their country than were those which the British were expecting them to fight.

For those who were caught supporting the British, the Germans inflicted severe punishment, not only on them as individuals but also on whole villages. At the same time, it was not uncommon for the various groups to savagely punish anyone from the other factions, and unsurprisingly this was especially the case with the Partisans who were already demonstrating the most ruthless, violent and oppressive manner in which they would later rule the country.

I make no excuse for briefly touching on these various issues in this essay which is aimed not at politics but at the bravery of the men operating in Albania during the War. I make no excuse because, as a former soldier myself, I can imagine something of the frustration and exasperation that those men must have felt as they repeatedly tried to achieve their extremely dangerous mission whilst working in such a confused and chaotic situation - chaotic and confused not only within Albania but also in their own chain of command through Bari to London.

FIGHTERS

Some foreigners, even to this day, have made inaccurate and ill-informed comments about the Albanians unwillingness to fight. From a purely British point of view this must be seen in the backdrop of the years of hard fighting in which they had already been involved around the world. I would strongly argue that many Albanians showed huge strength and bravery. It was *their* country, *their* villages, *their* wives, women, children and elderly who were the recipients of German (or Partisan) punitive responses to any sign of resistance.

It is interesting to read the various accounts of Special Operations Executive (SOE) operatives who wrote of their experiences in Albania. Usually once they had made contact with one of the three main factions they remained within that faction (with a few exceptions), and frequently they struck up strong bonds of respect and friendship. Yes, there were many frustrations, but bearing in mind the fundamentally different perspectives this is surely unsurprising. The best of the accounts express a deep attachment with the Albanians, and a frustration equally with their British controllers as with the local situation. Some of the British SOE officers were very outspoken and critical of the unforthcoming support from UK. Again, from personal experience I can relate with the great frustration they must have felt – it appears on one of my own annual personnel reports that I was "too enthusiastic" in my own efforts to generate interest and resources from London! I am very clear in my own mind that at an individual level, "on the ground", many of the more experienced SOE officers did indeed push as hard as they possibly could for more support to be given, and also to help the Albanian nationalist leaders, mindful of their likely fate at the hands of the communists once the British were extracted from the country.

Regardless of why, and remembering things from a purely British SOE perspective, it seemed that it was the Partisans who were most prepared to fight the Germans, and the British therefore supported them more strongly in accordance with the clearly stated policy to support whoever would fight the Germans – much as had been done in Malaya. One might deduce that the Partisans had more to gain and less to lose than the Legality Movement or Ballists, and those two groups had much more to lose if the Partisans were left in power at the end of the War. I would argue, that one may therefore sympathise with their desire for weapons to fight the communists as much, if not more, than fighting the Germans.

Photograph from the author's collection: "Smiley and Amery with Turkestanis".

SUPPRESSED REPORTS

I have briefly mentioned already that some of the deployed British officers, including Julian Amery and Billy McLean, believed that some of their reports intended for London, which described planned or actual anti-German operations by Zogist or Ballist groups, were deliberately suppressed or delayed in the SOE headquarters in Bari. They believed that there were Communist sympathisers or perhaps even agents within the headquarters.

Conversely, others, including Hibbert, insisted that the decision to cease support for all but the Partisans was made objectively based on actions taken against the Germans which, afterall, was the mission of SOE in Albania, not the internal politics of the country, rightly or wrongly (unlike in Malaya).

Roderick Bailey has studied this in great detail in his fascinating and intensely detailed book *The Wildest Province: SOE in the*

Land of the Eagle". He concludes that there were a couple of communist sympathisers within SOE, but he does not believe that they influenced British policy. A comment has been made that the rank of the officer most strongly suspected of being a communist sympathizer was not sufficiently senior enough to affect policy decisions. I disagree. In certain posts I held as a Major I was certainly drafting and influencing policy – albeit one needs to clearly express justification for one's decisions. From my own experience I would say that often British officers and soldiers are trusted and encouraged to make decisions at ranks considerably lower than in many other armies, and even more so when employed in niche areas of expertise.

In David Smiley's excellent book, "Albanian Assignment", he wrote: "While some of the officers in the Albaniann section of the SOE office were well-intentioned, if led astray by insidious Communist propaganda, others were Communist agents. One was an officer in the Albanian Section, and I was told he stood as an unsuccessful Communist candidate in the 1945 election. It was not surprising that on our return I overheard him refer to our mission as "Fascists". I was told by one of the secretaries that it was he who had prevented further transmission of McLean's signal [requesting permission to evacuate the mission's key Albanian interlocutors] to Mr. Eden, and that he had deliberately disposed of the message.

GERMANY RETREATING AND THE TRUE COLOURS OF THE PARTISANS CLEAR FOR ALL TO SEE

We should also accept that as 1944 wore on it was increasingly clear that Germany was in retreat, and their only interest in Albania was as an escape route northwards, and at the same time it was beyond doubt that it was the communists who were gaining power throughout the country. Again therefore, one can imagine the feelings of the Ballists and Zogists who needed support at just the time that the British policy was to withdraw all support from all but the Partisans.

With the perspective which I am trying to paint here it is worth pondering on a telegram which Hoxha sent to the Allied headquarters in which he declared that Gani Kryeziu and Abaz Kupi were collaborators and enemies and that they would be arrested and executed, and that the British officers attached to them would be treated as collaborators also. Some of these telegrams were published in his book *'Rreziku anglo-amerikan për Shqipërinë'* (*'The Anglo-American Threat to Albania"*).

Whilst, perhaps incredibly, Hoxha achieved his aim in seeing UK withdraw support for all but the Partisans, he also made enemies with two strong British officers who would be influential in UK's attitude towards his communist government in Albania after the war, Julian Amery (who had been working with Kupi) and David Smiley (who had also been working with the nationalist groups).

IGNORING POLITICS AND FOCUSSING ON INDIVIDUALS

But, as is the real aim of this account, considering the conditions and constant dangers which the British soldiers in Albania were facing at an individual level, try to imagine what effect such declarations from Hoxha, and subsequent changes to British policy, would result. And yet, according to all the accounts written, there doesn't seem to have been a single case of those men just "giving up". No matter, they continued with their missions as best they possibly could, with determination and intense bravery.

I would ask the reader to pause from the politics (from all sides) and instead to ponder on the bravery and determination of these men. Surely this brings one to a much greater level of admiration for what was happening amongst the British in Albania. Many of these British soldiers and officers were parachuted into Albania alone, or in groups of just two or three, or sometimes dropped at a remote coastline, or else crossed the border on foot. Even today, just to survive in the rugged mountains of the country is extremely difficult, let alone to find their way through the complexities of who to trust, with language difficulties, who to meet, how to coordinate action, and so on. There was no guaranteed resupply, and they were often grossly under-nourished. The Royal Air Force missions to drop supplies to the men on the ground were themselves fraught with danger. Reading the various accounts, the incredible bravery of those men is surely worthy of praise, leaving the murky politics out of the equation.

Weeks were sometimes spent in snow-bound and lice-ridden huts in the mountains, or in dark, damp caves on the coast. Dysentery, malaria, hepatitis, hypothermia, frost-bite and sometimes near starvation were commonplace occurrences, and that is without even mentioning the ever present threat of the Germans, nor the possibility of betrayal if locals supported a different faction, or saw it as a way of preserving their own safety.

There are many, many stories of these men's incredible bravery, almost beyond belief. One example was written by Seymour about the condition of Arthur Nicholls:

> *"When I located him he was more than half-starved, verminous, exhausted and gangrene had obtained a firm grip on his feet. He had also had an accident having fallen down a mountainside and his shoulder was dislocated.*
>
> *His feet were in an almost unbelievable condition. Both were festering masses and the only indication of where his toes were was where bare bones showed through the gangrened flesh."*

Seymour's report continues to say that despite his near starvation and intense pain, Nicholls' fighting spirit was unimpaired and he immediately started to discuss the plan for future missions. Sadly, he died of his wounds.

The following details are given in the London Gazette of 1st March 1946:

> *"Awarded the George Cross for most conspicuous gallantry in carrying out hazardous work in a very brave manner." Brigadier Nicholls parachuted into Albania in October 1943 as General Staff Officer to the Allied Military Mission which organised resistance activities. The Mission was attacked and broken up by the Germans in December and from then on Brigadier Nicholls lived as a fugitive in the open mountains in freezing weather. He continued leading the remnants of the Mission but was suffering from frostbite so severely that he ordered an inexperienced man to amputate both his legs without anesthetic. He was pulled over the mountains lying upon his greatcoat by two members of his party. He was determined to reach a British Mission to make his report upon which the course of the war in Albania would depend. He succeeded in this but had gone beyond the limits of endurance and died from gangrene and heart failure."*

In another incident a British radio operator was forced to watch one of the brave Albanian nationalists being tortured to death by a group of Partisans, with threats that they would do the same to him afterwards. Only at the last minute was his own life saved. Please do not misunderstand me, dear reader, it was far worse for the captured Albanians.

The British SOE soldiers and officers who deployed into Albania included some who were to become famous thereafter. Because of some of the larger-than-life characters involved it is easy to over-glamorize the whole SOE mission, but we must never forget the generally tough men, physically and mentally tough, who are less well known but were equally as brave and deserving of recognition. Nevertheless, to give a few examples of the characters involved it is hard not to give a line or two to some of the "big characters".

These included Bill Tilman who had fought in the First World War, including at the Battle of the Somme and was awarded the Military Cross for bravery, not once but twice. After the First World War he moved to Kenya to grow coffee, and it was there that he developed a mountaineering partnership with Eric Shipton. In 1929 they traversed Mount Kenya, then ascended Kilimanjaro and the fabled "Mountains of the Moon", Ruwenzori. When he decided to leave Africa, instead of simply flying out he rode a bicycle across the continent to the west coast before embarking on a ship for England. In the 1930s he was involved in two of the Everest expeditions, in the 1935 Reconnaissance Expedition and then as expedition leader in 1938 when he reached 27,200 feet, without oxygen. He volunteered for service in the Second World War and saw action in North Africa and Dunkirk before volunteering to serve with the SOE and being parachuted in to Albania. After the War was over, he took up deep sea sailing, voyaging to the Arctic and Antarctic, and in 1977, his 80th year, he was invited to be part of the crew aboard the converted steel tug *En Avant* with mountaineers sailing to the South Atlantic to climb Smith Island. En route to Rio de Janeiro the expedition disappeared without trace, never to be seen again.

Then there was Anthony Quayle who had studied dramatic art prior to World War Two and later became a famous actor and theatre director. As an actor he was frequently given the roles of the archetypal "decent British officer" in which he successfully drew on his own wartime experiences to add realism to the parts which other actors who had never been in such conditions could rarely achieve. He was nominated for an Oscar and a Golden Globe. It is said that his experiences in the SOE missions in Albania affected him greatly, but he disliked talking about it.

Alan Hare was the son of the fourth Earl of Listowel and educated at Eton and Oxford. After the Second World War, it is believed that he became a British spy before being appointed as the chairman of the British newspaper, the Financial Times, where he succeeded in turning it into a truly international newspaper. During his SOE time in Albania he was betrayed by Partisans and ambushed by the Germans. He suffered terrible frostbite in his escape across the snowy mountains and was later found by another SOE operative in a dingy cowshed, but recovering quite cheerfully, and talked of Oxford dinners, tours of Burgundy, and heated political discussions in London night-clubs, as if there was nothing untoward! He was later awarded the Military Cross.

And Peter Kemp must be mentioned - an extremely colourful maverick, staunch monarchist and conservative. He was studying law when, disturbed by the rise of communism, he left his studies in 1936 to fight for General Franco, joining the Spanish Legion. He was wounded several times but continued fighting until finally suffering a shattered jaw and badly damaged hands in a mortar attack. These injuries forced him to return to England, only to then become one of the first members of the SOE.

Reginald Hibbert later joined the British Foreign Office and served in Bucharest, Vienna, Guatemala, Ankara, Brussels, Mongolia, Singapore and Germany before returning to UK and achieving the post of Deputy Under-Secretary of State, Foreign and Commonwealth Office, prior to being appointed British Ambassador to France (1979-82).

Well known, and mentioned earlier in this account, is Julian Amery who would subsequently enter politics. Amery had been a war correspondent before the Second World War and later an Attaché in Belgrade. After commencement of the War he joined the Royal Air Force and attained the rank of sergeant before being commissioned and transferred to the Army where he reached the rank of captain. Initially he served in Malta and Yugoslavia before joining the SOE missions to Albania in 1943-44. He was convinced that the British government should support King Zog. Amery wrote clearly of his frustrations in trying to persuade London of the dreadful fate facing Albania otherwise. He became a close friend of King Zog and once described him as "the cleverest man I have ever met". In 1945 he moved to China and became the Prime Minister's Personal Representative to Genalissimo Chiang Kai-shek. On returning to UK he entered politics and served successfully as a Member of Parliament for an amazing 39 years between 1950 and 1992.

Perhaps one of the most well-known characters was David Smiley. During the Second World War he served in Palestine, Iraq, Persia, Syria, and the Western Desert before joining the SOE for operations in Albania and Thailand. His Regiment sailed for Palestine in 1939, and in 1940 he joined the Somaliland Camel Corps, but arrived the very day that orders were received to evacuate that country. He then moved to Egypt where he persuaded General Wavell, a family friend, to recommend him for service with the British Commandos which had only recently been formed. His first mission as a Commando company commander was to secretly enter Abyssinia from Sudan. In Syria he fought against the Vichy French. In 1943 he was recruited by the SOE and undertook his first operation with them in Palestine in the same year. Later in 1943 he parachuted into Albania where he coordinated partisan operations for eight months and was awarded the Military Cross for his actions. He was again parachuted into Albania in April with "Billy" McLean and was awarded a Bar to his Military Cross. His military career continued highly successfully after the end of World War Two, including a mission with the SOE in Thailand. Between 1955 – 58 he was appointed the British Military Attaché to Stockholm. He had a farm in Kenya and, unusually, represented them in the Commonwealth Winter Games of 1960. He was Commander of the Sultan of Muscat and Oman's Armed Forces between 1958 and 1961, and then between 1962 – 1967 became a Military Advisor to Yemen. I was fortunate to be invited to David's London home for afternoon tea once when I was back in UK and returned to him a number of his original photographs which he had taken during his operations in Albania, and which I had come by. With his permission I kept copies for myself. Sadly, David died not so long afterwards (January 2009) and I understand that his extensive photographic collection was passed to the Imperial War Museum in London.

So, above are a few paragraphs about some of the colourful characters involved with the SOE missions in Albania, but as previously stated, let the bravery of the rest not be over-shadowed by the colourful few. It is not possible to write in any detail about the many exploits of the officers and soldiers, and nor is that the aim of this brief account. My intention is simply to ask the reader to remember the different national perspectives before judging one side or the other. Also, as I always wished to do when I was living in Albania, I hope to have expressed something of the individual bravery of those involved, regardless of politics. Repeating myself, nor do I wish in any way to undermine the bravery which many Albanians demonstrated, and one may justifiably argue that in some cases the Albanian bravery, especially considering what was at stake for them and their families and communities, was greater than anyone else's.

NON-SOE MISSIONS

There were also some non-SOE missions during which British servicemen lost their lives on Albanian soil.

RAF CASUALTIES FLYING OVER ALBANIA

On 28 October 1940, Italian forces invaded south into Greece from occupied Albania. The Greek Army initially managed to stand firm against the attack. Commonwealth troops redeployed from Egypt to assist, but this could not be achieved until March 1941. On the 6th of April a German invasion of mainland Greece quickly overwhelmed the Allied forces. They were evacuated by the Royal Navy, mostly to the strategically important island of Crete.

On the morning of 20th May 1941, the Germans launched an airborne assault against the British, Australian, New Zealand and Greek forces and quickly captured Maleme airfield and after some days the Allies were forced to evacuate by sea. German air and sea attacks continued to attack the retreating forces, inflicting many casualties. In total the Royal Navy lost three cruisers and six destroyers and a further 16 vessels suffered heavy damage. The evacuation was complete by 1st June 1941. The Battle for Crete was certainly a German victory, but they also suffered heavy losses with approximately 4,000 killed or missing, and this would be the last time that they would attempt a major airborne assault. Out of the 32,000 Commonwealth forces in Crete, approximately 18,000 were evacuated, and 12,000 were taken prisoner and a further 2,000 were killed. I briefly mention this here because some Royal Air Force men lost their lives over Albanian territory as a result of these operations.

ROYAL MARINES - SPILJE

Another non-SOE operation was an attempt to assist Albanian partisans to attack the German garrison at Spilje. 250 men, mainly from No.2 Commando Royal Marines, landed at Spilje on the night of 28th/29th July 1944 with an objective to attack a German position near the village of Himare. This they did and estimated that 100 Germans had been killed, whilst 29 of their own men lost their lives and 61 were wounded. It has been said that the bravery and indeed audacity of the British attack, with a four-mile approach across difficult terrain, to attack a strongly fortified German position advantageously located on a high ridge, showing great discipline and careful planning including a strict time limit, was greatly inspiring for the Partisans.

ROYAL MARINES - SARANDA

The other non-SOE mission, again using No.2 Commando, aimed to capture the port of Saranda from the Germans who were using it to support their garrison on the Greek island of Corfu. The Commando landed on a beach just under 10 kilometers north of Saranda on 22 September, and soon came under artillery fire. They had been told that 200 Germans were located in Saranda, only to discover that the actual figure was closer to 2000!

Reinforcements were urgently sent from No. 40 (Royal Marine) Commando, arriving on 24 September, after which the British were able to successfully capture Saranda by the 9th October. As a result the Germans on Corfu could not be resupplied and were forced to surrender.

THE WAR ENDS

In bringing this to a close I reluctantly feel the necessity to return to politics, but I wish the reader to consider these final comments directly to the actions of the British in Albania throughout their involvement during the War.

At the 28th November 1944 military victory parade, Colonel Palmer (the then Head of the British Mission) along with the American, Thomas Stefan, appeared on the podium alongside the victorious Hoxha. It seems impossible that the British (and Americans) were not aware of the communists' savage retributions which were already being inflicted against Ballists, Zogists, and anyone else who opposed them. Indeed, many atrocities had been witnessed firsthand. And yet there is evidence that there were still hopes that after the War Albania would have free and fair democratic elections.

Perhaps in a final diplomatic effort Hoxha was invited for dinner with the British Head of Mission, General Hodgson, in September 1945. As is usually the case at seemingly "social" diplomatic events there was a reason behind the invite, and in this case it was to try to persuade Hoxha to allow opposition parties to stand in the elections which were scheduled to take place a couple of months thereafter. According to Hoxha's account of the dinner he completely rebuffed the British attempts, telling them that the War had already settled the future of the country.

This was the last time that Hoxha would visit a western Embassy in Albania for the rest of his life, and if the British were in any illusion about Albania becoming a democratic and friendly ally surely this was now well and truly shattered for the next 47 years. I will not stray into a discussion of the Corfu Straits incident as I discuss that elsewhere, but suffice to say that the British diplomatic staff were the first to leave Albania in 1946, with the Americans following a few weeks later.

Whilst wishing this to be a short note to pay tribute to the bravery of the British and Commonwealth men who were active in Albania during World War Two, I have found it necessary, reluctantly, to repeatedly return to the politics and wider picture, because only from doing so can we begin to understand why things were as they were.

It is so easy for us to sit in our nice cozy armchairs and criticize, and by that I mean foreigners criticizing Albanians for not fighting the occupiers with greater determination, just as equally as Albanians criticizing the British for not doing more and for seemingly not caring about the future post-War consequences of their decisions. During my time in Albania I had many discussions with Albanians about the sensitive issue of Britain's involvement in World War Two. As they had suffered from the most severe oppression of decades of extreme communism, and with the effects of that still continuing, I could understand why some continued to feel betrayed, and in my heart I sympathized. Trying to remain faithful to the country of my birth I often reminded those Albanians who argued with me that at least the British had tried to do *something,* more than any other country. I reminded them that the British were not the invaders who had created this situation in the first place, and nor were the British party to plans to carve up Albania, as was the intention of some.

Only if we attempt to understand the wider situation, the politics behind it all, the Albanians understandably and rightly more concerned about the longer-term situation for them and their country, and for the war-weary British concerns to defeat the Germans without getting embroiled in local politics, does it begin to make sense.

But in my final line, having emphasized the need to see the wider picture, I ask the reader once more to put all that aside and to simply ponder on the British soldiers as individuals, those highly motivated men, trying to achieve the mission that they were given, in the most difficult and dangerous of circumstances.

Allow me to quote again from Smiley's book, "Albanian Assignment":

> *"To this day I am ashamed of this abandonment of our friends. On our return we learnt that our orders to do so were simply to appease Enver Hoxha and his fellow murders, this made our feelings more bitter.*
>
> *Our departure is a bad memory of the sad farewells to those of our friends who knew the secret that we were going. On security grounds we had to conceal it from the others, slipping off at night without a word."*

When I met David Smiley so many years later, I can say first hand that his sentiments regarding this had not changed throughout the remainder of his life.

Surely, all politics aside, these are worthy of our respect as men of immense bravery. I hope that the late Julian Amery would not mind me quoting from his excellent book, "The Sons of the Eagle – A Study in Guerilla War":

> *We failed; and not the least of the causes of our failure was our seeming impotence as a nation to proclaim a new faith which the stricken peoples of Europe might have turned. In the dark days when we had stood alone, England had fired the world by her example, and men had believed that we might fashion a new order out of the furnace of war. As victory drew on, their hopes receded, and others stepped in to claim the prize for which we had toiled. Much of our work, above all in the Balkans, was swept away in "the gale of the world". Yet I do not believe that we worked in vain.*

The weakness or the error of our policies will be forgotten or forgiven with the lapse of time, but the peoples will long remember the British officers and men who came to them out of the sea and down from the sky, to share their hardships in the hour of need. These only did their duty, but in so doing they sowed a seed; and one day there will be a harvest."

Julian Amery
Eaton Square, London,
November 4, 1947

(See Annex C for a list of British deaths.)

EDITH DURHAM

Edith Durham (1863 – 1944) was a British traveler, artist and writer, most famous for her accounts of life in Albania in the early 20th century. I read a number of her books before moving to Albania, and still enjoy re-reading them today, and so simply most include something about her.

Edith was born in the prestigious Hanover Square in London, her father being a well-known surgeon. She was the eldest of nine children and studied at the Royal Academy of Arts.

After her father died, as the eldest daughter, she became responsible for caring for her sick mother. As she wrote in one of her books,

> *"Completely exhausted by constant attendance on an invalid relative, the future stretched before me as endless years of grey monotony, and escape seemed hopeless."*

The family doctor realized the tole that these duties were having on Edith and insisted that she took at least two months holiday a year,

> *"Take them in quite a new place. Get right away no matter where, so long as the change is complete."*

And so it was that at the age of 37 Edith took a sea trip along the Dalmatian coast with a female friend. She then continued to Cetinje, the capital of Montenegro, and, as she wrote,

> *"It was in Cetinje that it was borne in on me that I had found the "quite new place" which I sought."*

Her life would never be the same again.

From there she traveled to Podgoritza which is where she had her first contact with Albanians. She then traveled to Trebinje, Sarajevo and Mostar, before returning to Trieste on the Dalmation coast.

In 1902-03 this brave woman traveled through Serbia and studied the language as well as Balkan history, the result of which was her first book, "*Through the Lands of the Serbs*", first published in 1904. She also visited Kosovo and Shkodra – rare visits in those times. It still amazes me to read about her traveling alone into such a relatively unknown part of the world, and at that period in history.

Towards the end of 1903 she returned to Montenegro for a five-month stay. It was at this time that she also made her first lengthy visit to Albania. Edith described her experience of the conditions she witnessed in her book, "*The Burden of the Balkans*", published in London in 1905.

The next three summers were spent traveling through Montenegro, Bosnia and Herzegovina, all the time deepening her intimate knowledge of the Balkan region. What she saw as dislikable Serbian nationalism was raging across the region, and the resultant suffering of other ethnic groups in those lands, especially the Albanians, caused her to turn away from Serbia and to focus her attention on Albania and her people. Supporters of the idea of a Yugoslav state strongly criticized Edith as her interest and support of Albania deepened. She was equally critical of them, and especially their intentions to annex Albanian populated parts of Kosovo. She criticized the Serbs and their supporters (in UK and elsewhere) for creating, in effect, a greater Serbia which historically she claimed had never existed despite claims to the contrary, and resulted in unfair and harsher rule for the Albanian populations in those regions than was ever previously the case under the Ottomans.

In 1908 she traveled from Montenegro to Shkodra, and from there through the Albanian highlands. The literary product of this was her book, "*High Albania*", published in 1909, and which became her most widely read book. Still today it is highly regarded as probably the best account of Albanian highland life at that period of history. I remember being fascinated when I first read it, and I highly recommend it to anyone with an interest in this part of the world. Perhaps surprisingly for such a male dominated society, Edith was to be highly regarded, trusted, and respected by the northern Albanians, who nicknamed her, "*Mbretëresha e Malësoreve*", or "Kraljica e

Malesorëvet" ("Queen of the Highlanders") and to this day her name is well known in northern Albania. On my own frequent trips to the northern mountainous regions, when I introduced myself as an Englishman smiles and the words "Edith Durham" often followed as if they had personally known her. She travelled unmolested across the Highlands.

Her next book was *"The Struggle for Scutari"* which was published in London in 1914 and described the Montenegrin siege of Shkodra after the declaration of Albanian independence. At this time she also visited Vlora in the south, but found that conditions were no better there due to the aggression of the Greeks who sought territorial gains into Albanian territory. She wrote extremely strongly about atrocities committed against the Albanians by the Greeks, with villages systematically burnt and Albanians forced to flee. She also wrote of all sorts of incredible trickery intended to prove to the international community that whole areas of southern Albania were in fact Greek. Some of what she wrote is certainly corroborated in the official accounts of international visits to the disputed areas when the "Great Powers" were deciding international borders.

She was forced to leave Albania at the outbreak of the First World War in 1914 and sailed to Spain to work in a hospital in Biscay, and later for the YMCA in Egypt.

In 1920 Edith published *"Twenty Years of Balkan Struggle"* which was a summary of her experiences and is another excellent and fascinating book. Her last visit was a year later but growing health issues curtailed more travel thereafter, although she remained a supporter and champion of the Albanian people for the remainder of her life. She was one of the founding members of the Anglo-Albanian Association in London, and she continued to write many letters and articles for magazines and newspapers about the Balkans, often correcting ill-informed prejudices. In 1925 she published what was perhaps her most controversial book, *"The Serajevo Crime"* which considered the background of the Sarajevo assassination which was the catalyst for the start of the First World War.

When she died in 1944, the exiled King Zog of the Albanians praised her highly, writing,

> *"She gave us her heart and she won the ear of our mountaineers."*

Even in 2004 the then Albanian President Moisiu described her as,

> *"one of the most distinguished personalities of the Albanian world during the last century".*

Reading her books one can feel her genuine affection for the Albanian people. She was not, as some critics have accused, blind to faults and weaknesses, and these can also be read in her fascinating accounts if those critics bothered to read them! Nevertheless, her understanding and love of the Albanian Highlands, and the many colourful characters she met along the way, is clear for all to read.

I am currently reading her accounts of the Albanian uprisings which began in 1910 against the occupying Turks, and the stories of the bravery of many of the Albanian Highlanders of the time is amazing. But conversely the failure of the European countries to come to Albania's aide, and in some cases outright treachery, is hard to swallow. So many Albanians simply could not understand why the European countries would stand by and do nothing. I am attempting to ensure that this book is uncontroversial, as far as can be, but I simply must write that I was often highly frustrated when I did all I could to engender interest and support in my own work in Albania, but all too often without any positive response. Of course, such things change over time, sometimes rapidly, and I was always aware that some Albanians I was working with must have felt that I was not trying hard enough because otherwise why wouldn't support they had enjoyed previously not be forthcoming. If only they knew how hard I was trying! Indeed, I was criticized on one of my own annual performance reports for being "too enthusiastic" and "trying too hard"! So, I am not as surprised as many others might be at the lack of engagement from London and other

Powers of which Edith frequently wrote, sad though it is to admit that. Policies change like the wind sometimes, economy and other political factors being the *real politik.*

In closing this short chapter on Edith Durham I wish to quote from her book, "Twenty Years of Balkan Tangle", taking up from where she has been describing Turk and Greek efforts to ban the Albanian language from being taught or appearing in print, and even the Austrian efforts in the north to print religious books in Albanian but,

> *".....with the intent of winning over the Northern Christians to Austria, and was directed rather to dividing the Christians from the Moslems, and to weakening rather than strengthening the sense of Albanian nationality."*

She wrote:

> *"None of these efforts on the part of Albania's enemies killed the strong race instinct which has enabled the Albanian to survive the Roman Empire and the fall of Byantium, outlive the fleeting mediaeval Empires of Bulgar and Serb, and finally emerge from the wreck of the mighty Ottoman Empire, retaining his language, his customs and his primitive vigour – a rock over which the tides of invasion have washed in vain."*

In Edith's final paragraph in this same book, she wrote,

> *"At the moment of going to press the Serbs have made a wanton attack on North Albania from three points. But they will not kill the spirit of the Albanian people, who have resisted denationalization for a thousand years, and who beg only for the right to take their place in the Balkans and live in freedom and harmony with their neighbours, and who now, at the time of going to press are fighting bravely for Liberty.*

I will not write Finis, for the tale of the Balkan tangle does not end here."

And how right she was, and she wrote that in 1920!

THE BRIDGE
(TRAVELING ALONGSIDE THE RIVER MAT)

Some weeks previously, I had been exploring the central-eastern part of the country and returning home to Tirana I had driven alongside part of the River Mat (Lumi Mat). I was stunned by its glorious ruggedness and determined to return again at a more leisurely pace.

I was so impressed with the natural beauty that I read all that I could find about the area. The River Mat stretched from the northeast for 115 kilometres, flowing roughly southwest until it meets the river Fan, and then into the Adriatic Sea. The River Fan was formed from two sources: the Great Fan (Fan i Madh) and the Little Fan (Fan i Vogël), and they joined near the town of Rrëshen, before meeting up with the Mat, east of the town of Milot.

Higher up, over the centuries the Mat has eroded the landscape to form the most beautiful gorges and canyons, as beautiful as may be found anywhere in the world. Its source is found in the mountains in Martanesh, Dibër County, in the east of the country. Since 2015, the 1900 or so residents of Martanesh have become a subdivision of the municipality of Bulqizë. The majority of the population are from the Bektashi faith of which I briefly mention elsewhere in this book, with a small Catholic minority.

From Martanesh the Mat winds its way westwards to the municipality of Mat and through the towns of Klos and Burrel. And it was towards Burrel, just over 90 kilometers from Tirana, that I was traveling, and the area around *Liqeni i Ulzës* – ("Lake Ulëz"), which is actually a reservoir.

My friendship with the late King Leka Zogu made me want to head for Burrel - known by some as the "Land of Kings", the birthplace of Ahmet Zogolli, King Leka's father, in 1895. He became Prime Minister of Albania between 1922 and 1924, and President between 1925 – 1928. Notice, that means that he was

Prime Minister at age 27 and President when he was only 30. He then became the first King of the Albanians, King Ahmet Zogu, from 1928. Some critics smile and sneer that he was not really of royal descent. All I would say is that all royal dynasties started at some point in time, and he was a powerful and influential clan leader. The Great Powers had tried to inflict an outsider on the country, the Prussian Prince Wilhelm of Wied. One should understand that despite the growing Albanian nationalism there was no unified government, and all of Albania's neighbours were trying to grab Albanian land for themselves which, had they been successful, would have carved up Albania completely, leaving nothing left. The intention was therefore to install a Prince who could unify the country and thus defend it as a sovereign State. Wilhelm lasted 6 months – February to September 1914, giving up the task shortly before the outbreak of the First World War. Some claim everything was stacked against him and made it nigh on impossible for him to succeed, but others have stated that he was simply too weak, didn't understand the country and the Albanian people, and was too frightened to leave Durres! Ahmet Zogu by comparison was head of a clan, well known as a strong leader despite his young age, and incredibly brave.

Here is an interesting story about King Zog's family home in Bernard Newman's 1938 book, "Albanian Journey":

> *They* [the villagers] *told me a stirring tale of the burning of the house by the Yugoslavs in 1920. When the Yugoslavs arrived, Zog was away in the south fighting against the Italians. So his mother and sister got busy on the Albanian "telephone"* [calling out from one mountain side to the next], *and the shrill cries down the valley called out every available man to defend their land. Most of the men were already with Zog, and there were only old men and boys left. Even the boys of Albania are skilled with the rifle, however, and they put up such a strong resistance that the Yuogslavs were held back until Zog arrived with his army."*

As I have attempted to emphasise throughout this book, as we sit judgmental in our cosy armchairs, it is important to put things in their proper context of time and place. In this case, should we really believe that a Prussian nobleman with little knowledge of Albania, and no connection to it, without the strength and bravery to even travel around the country, let alone the understanding of the people to unite them, should have been accepted as a true Prince of Albania, whereas a strong and respected Albanian clan leader should not? It is so easy to look back so many decades later and accuse and criticize, but put in the context of time and place, and with Serbia, Montenegro, Italy, Bulgaria, Austria, and Greece all desirous of seizing Albanian territory and annihilating the country in the process, things might seem somewhat different.

It is claimed that the Zogu Family are direct descendants of the national hero, Skanderbeg. We should also look carefully at the country before Ahmet Zogu assumed the throne and assess what he achieved. There were virtually no roads, precious few schools, and with a very high rate of illiteracy. Blood feuds were rampant. Moslem women (and even some Christian women) wore full veils. Feelings of nationalism as an independent country were generally struggling to find their way in a unifying fashion with various characters vying for egotistical power rather than for the benefit of the country and Albanian people. Because of the constant and very real threats from all its neighbours, and the all too often less than fair, or honest, interventions of the larger European countries, Albania was the last of the Balkan countries to rid itself of its Ottoman rulers as many Albanians realized that the country's very existence was more assured with the Turks than without.

Ahmet Zogu developed an efficient police force, initially using British police officers to advise and lead. (There had previously been less successful attempts, before Zogu's time, to use the Dutch in this role.) He embarked on a road building programme and all main towns became linked by roads for the very first time. Many schools were opened, the veil was banned, and the rule of law became paramount rather than the ancient family feuding. In the capital city boulevards and government buildings were built. All too often these are claimed to be from the Italian occupation period, but please check the dates, dear read, most were from King Zog's rule, or some were planned but not finished before the Italian invasion. In 1938 He opened Albania's borders to thousands of Jews facing Nazi occupation, and the Albanian people welcomed them and in many cases faced considerable personal dangers in harboring and supporting them in the greatest traditions of Albanian hospitality for the guest.

King Ahmet Zogu has been criticized by some for the financial reliance on the Italians, and concessions demanded by them, but clearly the country needed money from somewhere in order to modernize, and requests for assistance from other countries came to naught. The progress that was made in a remarkably short space of time was considerable. Sadly, He was forced into exile when the Italians invaded the day after the birth of His son, Leka Zogu, in 1939. Again, some have criticized Him for leaving, but this was not unusual at the time. London became home to many Royal families and leaders from across Europe who had fled their own countries at the outbreak of war, not through cowardice, but pragmatism - what is the use of a dead monarch? I discussed this exile with King Leka during a relaxing afternoon in His villa and I was convinced beyond any doubt that the motivation was that having got His family to safety, King Ahmet, (King Leka's father, and grandfather of the current Crown Prince Leka II), would be able to more effectively organize resistance against the invaders from a free country, rather than what might have been His fate should He have attempted to remain in Albania. I discuss this briefly in the chapter on the British in Albania in World War Two. Disappointingly, for whatever reason, the British did not support King Zog, and his many offers to personally organize and even lead an attack back into Albania were always refused. Of his bravery, and that of his son, King Leka, with whom I shared many happy times, there is absolutely no question. When I was living and working in Albania, Crown

Prince Leka II attended the prestigious Royal Military Academy Sandhurst, from where I had been commissioned some years earlier. On successful completion of the course Crown Prince Leka was awarded the coveted King Hussein medal. Be in no doubt, this is a tough course and one's family background carries no influence – indeed, it might make the instructing staff test the cadet even more rigorously. I speak from personal experience – when I was attending the Academy there was a Middle Eastern Prince from a very wealthy and influential family in my platoon, but he was deemed not to have succeeded and was back-termed, even though he had reached the very end of the course. This is a genuinely testing course for anyone, regardless of background. I remember being so thrilled when I received the telephone call from the Academy to inform me of Prince Leka's wonderful achievement!

As I have allowed myself to disappear on this tangent, please allow me dear reader to quote from Tajar Zavalani's excellent "History of Albania" which was edited by Robert Elsie and Bejtullah Destani:

> *It is still early to make a definitive appreciate appreciation of King Zog's role in Albanian history period. We must leave that to future historians with full access to the archives. The present author's modest opinion, based on 30 years in Albanian politics, is that Zog was the man of destiny at this stage of Albania's evolution. Albania had tried the experiment of a foreign monarch and it had not worked. The conditions existed for building a truly democratic state after the revolution of June 1924, but failed lamentably. Admittedly, the nation was not politically mature, and its leaders lacked the experience and the discipline of a freely organized party system required to make democracy success. Equally the government that issued from the revolution was unable to enforce the kind of benevolent, enlightened dictatorship that Mustafa Kemal Ataturk was exercising so successfully in Turkey. The consolidation of the state within its newly fixed frontiers was historically*

the most urgent task, and Ahmet Zogu happened to be the only man capable of carrying it out. He had his limitations, conditioned by his background, his upbringing and his incomplete education, which made it impossible for him to grasp the economic and social problems of a modern state. His personal shortcomings were aggravated by the refusal or inability of the League of Nations to provide the financial assistance, which would have helped Albania stand on its own feet without becoming a sphere of influence for any of its neighbors. He chose Italy as a lesser evil, but then allowed it to acquire a predominant economic position by grossly mismanaging the financial help he received. On balance he succeeded in safeguarding the political independence of the country to the very end of the interwar period. Consequently, Mussolini had to invade Albania with a colossal display of armed force before he could use the country as a pawn in his imperialistic game.

Julian Amery, who I mention in the chapter, "The British in Albania in World War Two", educated at Eton and Oxford, and who had an interface with many world leaders of the time, wrote in his 1973 book, *Approach March*, (published by Hutchinson) that King Ahmet Zogu was, *"the cleverest man I have met"*.

All I would add to the above quotations, and repeating myself, is an urging to remember how incredibly young Ahmet Zogu was: Prime Minister at age 27, President at the age of 30, and King at age 33. He was still only 44 when forced into exile, and yet look how far he developed the country in that short time. Then consider the regression that occurred throughout the next 5 decades until the end of the communist regime. How different it all could have been. Finally, before closing this diversion, from my personal experience, I was left without any doubts about the pure motivation of the late King Leka I, and of Crown Prince Leka II, to help Albania and the Albanian people. I do not want to stray into political systems however – that is for the Albanian people to decide what best suits them and their circumstances.

Burrel was also the birthplace of Gjon Kastrioti, the father of Gjergj Kastrioti, better known as the national hero, Skanderbeg, and as mentioned above, it is claimed that the Zogu family were direct descendants. Burrel, now with a population of nearly 11,000, had been the birthplace of many famous Albanians including Tarhoncu Ahmed Pasha, a Grand Vizier of the Ottoman Empire, several footballers, actors and singers, and other well-known personalities.

I know I am disappearing off on all sorts of tangents with this story, dear reader, but I can't help myself. The history and culture of Albania is so rich and fascinating, and all these thoughts were flooding my mind as I drove along at a leisurely pace, simply admiring the most beautiful views. Honestly speaking I don't exactly know why I have these almost dream like experiences in Albania, well, not daydreams but inexplicable feelings of time standing still and simply feeling completely relaxed and at home. On such perfect days as this, especially when I had no particular schedule, no appointments, no time to keep, and no fixed destination, this same illogical but wonderful feeling was a frequent occurrence in Albania, more than anywhere else I have ever lived. It was a feeling of timelessness, of history past, present and future, a feeling of belonging to the landscape I was so in love with, a feeling of "now". Does that sound illogical and over-romantic when I am talking so much about history? Well, I did say it was "illogical", in more ways than one!

But history is alive, it is not something dead in the past, something to be buried and forgotten. It helps define who we are today, collectively and individually, whether we like it or not. It is not always good, not always the history we would choose in our perfect imaginations. I do not mean to suggest for a second that we should stand still, that this was our ancestors' past and therefore we are stuck forever. No, things change, things must change, but we must change for the better. We must create our own part of history with honour and integrity so that future generations will look back at us with respect, and our ancestors would be proud of our efforts. What we do today is tomorrow's history.

Another tangent to this story, but all I will offer in my defense for these side-tracks, is that this is what was in my mind as yet another Range Rover shot past me, nearly pushing me off the side of the road, the driver clearly believing that he was someone special, more important than me or anyone else on the road. Well excuse me you fool, but I have more respect for the honest old man with his donkey, living his life with decency, honour, and tradition. He would be the man who would welcome me to his home, and he would be the man whose hand I would be honoured to shake. The egotistical, selfish oaf in the flashy car - sorry to disappoint you whoever you were - but I have seen many more like you than I care to remember. You are just another empty shell, chasing rainbows, the same as can be found anywhere in the world, no better, no worse.

Let's get back to this journey – archaeologists have discovered proof of human habitation in this area right back to the Middle Paleolithic era (Middle Stone Age) – probably sometime in the middle of the third millennium BC. The tribe of Pirustae resisted the Roman invasion in this area until the second century BC.

In more recent times Burrel was well-known for its apple-tree lined streets but sadly during Communist days and the years of unrest which immediately followed, almost all the trees were cut down and now very few apple trees can be seen. I hope that one day some enlightened leader will undertake an apple tree replanting programme, and that the local population will treasure such a move. So rather than being famous for apple trees, Burrel became known as a miners' town during communist days. Now all the mines are closed except, I understand, for a ferrochrome plant.

This glorious historical town became a refugee camp which housed about 2,000 people who had fled from the Serbian atrocities in Kosovo. Here is an example of the history I mentioned – we would prefer it could be re-written differently and that the terrible events in Kosovo had never happened, but this sad story is part of our more modern history, and we forget such things at our peril. We move on, but we don't forget, not because we always want to hate and not build bridges, but because if we do forget such events can all too easily reoccur.

Much less glorious was one of the most infamous prisons of the communist regime which was located in Burrel. As was far too common in the country in the darkest of years, many ordinary people, religious figures, and anyone with even a hint of political disagreement, were locked up in the most dreadful of conditions. In Burrel there were quite a number of well-known personalities locked away, including the Catholic priest Dom Simon Jubani. He was jailed for 26 years, kept in a 3.6 x 7.2 metre cell with 30 other prisoners and frequently brutally beaten. Dom Simon was born in Shkodër and ordained in 1958 after which he served at the Abbey of Mirëdita. He was arrested in 1963. Dom Simon was later to write a memoir called "Burgjet e mia" (My Prison). Dom Simon was eventually released on the 13th of April 1989, along with other imprisoned Catholic priests, and on the 11th of November 1990, defying the still extant law, became the first priest to openly celebrate the first public Mass since the fall of Hoxha's regime.

Another famous inmate was Pjetër Arbnori whose father was killed whilst fighting the Partisans during the Second World War. He was jailed for 28 years at the age of 26. When his sentence was nearly complete another ten years was added to his sentence. It is hard to imagine the psychological effect that would result from such cruel treatment – one would need to be an extremely strong character to emerge unscathed. Eventually, in 1989, he was released, aged 54. He then worked as an apprentice to a carpenter. One might well presume that after 28 years in such dreadfully degraded conditions he would be a broken man and, at best, would then wish to quietly go about whatever remained of his life unnoticed. But what an incredible inner-strength and conviction he must have had because, less than five months after his release from Burrel jail, he actively participated in the anti-communist demonstration in Shkodër, during which Stalin's statue was pulled down by the crowd. In the first free elections Arbnori, was elected to Parliament, a feat which was repeated in three more elections. Twice he was elected to the position of Chairman of the Parliament of Albania and was also acting President in April 1992. When his Party lost the elections to the Socialist Party led by Fatos Nano in 1997 he believed that the State control and censorship that had been the norm in the Communist years could re-surface. The final straw was when the state-owned television station refused to air political broadcasts and news of policies of the opposition party. Arbnori went on hunger strike to draw attention to what was going on. He became known as the "Mandela of the Balkans" and attracted the attention of many western governments who put pressure on the Albanian parliament to guarantee the independence of the press from State interference. This became known as "the Arbnori Amendment".

After the end of the grim days of communism the prison at Burrel was closed and turned into a museum, but in 1997 Sali Berisha re-opened it as a prison.

So, how were these thoughts in my mind on such a beautiful day? It was that fool in his Range Rover, demanding to be respected when no respect was due, and four lines from the famous Bob Dylan song, "Hurricane":

> *Now all the criminals in their coats and their ties*
> *Are free to drink martinis and watch the sun rise*
> *While Rubin sits like Buddha in a ten-foot cell*
> *An innocent man in a living hell*

Anyhow, I let these darker thoughts disappear as I pulled into a nice little restaurant on the side of the reservoir. Time was drifting by and whilst it was my intention not to rush but simply to enjoy the breath-taking scenery, I realized that thoughts of exploring Burrel would have to wait for another time. And now I must offer the reader my sincere apologies. Names of places regarding this story, when I eventually stop disappearing down all these rabbit holes and settle down to tell the tale, have disappeared from my memory. I have tried to find them on a map, but the maps I have now are so much better than I had then, and some of the roads have definitely changed beyond recognition, and I just cannot identify where I was. I apologise, especially to those people involved in the rest of this story. I seem to remember the restaurant was called "Bar/Restaurant Kosova", but I might be wrong. Anyhow, it was on the old road from Skuraj to Burrel which crosses the lake which was created by the construction of the Shkopet hydropower plant. I believe the restaurant was in Shkopet where the road curved sharply. What is not in any doubt is that the landscape was absolutely beautiful. The water stretched out in front of the restaurant and a few tables were perfectly placed to enjoy the views, and rugged hills and imposing mountains perfectly framed the vista. The owner, whose name I sadly also cannot recall, came out and we chatted in Albanian for a while. He explained that his family had lived in this area for generations. I may be wrong, but he didn't seem desperate to leave, not trying to make money to escape to the city as so many others desired. He was proud of this area, proud of his ancestral heritage. I immediately liked him. I am all too aware that it is easy as an outsider to see these situations in a romantic way, not fully understanding the realities of the harshness of such life, but I sincerely felt that, providing he was making sufficient money to look after himself and his family, he would be happier here than anywhere. I hope that is true.

We chatted some more, and I explained that I was a vegetarian. As everywhere else I travelled in Albania, even in the most remote places, I was never made to feel that this was anything troublesome, something to mock as might happen in many places. I remember once driving down the Pacific Coast Highway in California and pulling off to a small restaurant. When I said I was vegetarian and anything without meat or fish would be great, I was stared at as if I had declared I had landed from Mars! What a contrast to my experiences in Albania. This fine young gentleman immediately suggested what he could prepare for me to eat. He did, and it was delicious!

We sat inside his small restaurant, the only customers, and enjoyed yet another delicious meal with fresh salad, tomatoes, cheese, yoghurt and freshly baked bread, and then sat outside next to the reservoir with a coffee. I could have sat there all afternoon chatting and listening to stories of his ancestors and the changes he had seen in the area. It was already too late for me to reach Burrel, but I had seen on my maps a bridge which would cross the flowing water and enable me to drive back to the main Shkodra-Tirana road on the other side of the river before it got dark. So, having been given one of his fossilized stone gathered from the local hills, I said I had to go. I still have that stone!

The author taking a break outside "Bar/Restaurant Kosova".

I followed the old Albanian military map carefully but there seemed to be nothing but a small track leading towards the river from the main road. Surely this couldn't be it. Could I have made a map-reading mistake? Unlikely – I was confident – and over-confidence is always a dangerous thing! Anyhow, I decided to turn around and see if I had somehow missed another minor road in accordance with my old map. I tracked back three or four hundred metres – no, that little track, with overgrown bushes overhanging it HAD to be the road I could see on the map. As I was wrestling with this I saw an older man, cigarette in hand, watching me from a little way further down the road, so went to speak to him. After the usual greetings I asked where the bridge was which would take me to the other side of the river. The old man clearly said,

> *"There is no bridge!"*
> *"Yes, isn't it down that narrow road there?"*
> *"No, no bridge."*
> *"There is definitely a bridge."*

How could I have been so stubborn to think that I might be right and a local could be unaware of a bridge? With hindsight it is of course ridiculous. But still I was adamant, and as stubborn as a donkey! I had to continue down the road to find a place where I could turn the car around, and as I did so I saw someone else. The same thing – almost the same conversation – *"there is no bridge"* - and still I didn't listen!

I turned my vehicle around and very, very carefully used all my map reading skills to verify every detail. I was even more sure that the small track I had seen had to be the one leading to the bridge. It had to be! I gingerly turned into the overgrown narrow lane, and it was clear that no vehicle had been down it for some time. But lo and behold, after a few hundred metres, there it was – an old iron bridge! OK, I admit it, I could see that it hadn't been used for a while. In good military fashion I got out and checked it for safety. It was not in the finest condition, but nor were a lot of places I travelled! 'Proceed with caution' was my decision. I must admit that I sighed a loud sigh of relief once safely over, but there was that idiotic part of me which kept patting myself on the back, *"I knew there was a bridge"*! Ridiculous!

There was a track leading perpendicular to the dilapidated old bridge facing west – all correct according to the map. Turn left, hah, I knew I was right!

Within a few hundred metres the track started to become narrower and narrower, but worse was the tall hump running down the centre. I could hear the bottom of the vehicle scraping. And it was only getting worse. And the sun was going down. And there was no way I could turn around. And there was no mobile phone reception.   And I hadn't brought the satellite phone with me.....and did I say already.....it was getting darker by the minute. I could only drive at less than walking speed, bang, scrape, eeek, no turning back – I had to go forward. At least I knew I was heading in the right direction, east to west, but the track no longer looked anything like it appeared on the map.

Darkness had fallen and everything was pitch black with not a light to be seen except from the twinkling stars overhead. This vehicle needed a couple of inches more road clearance as it was now scraping the bottom constantly. If it became stuck I don't know what I could do: no accurate idea of my precise location, and no cell phone coverage even if I did know, no light, no sign of habitation.   I was worried that I might rip something off the underside of the car if I attempted to reverse – I just had to keep the momentum forward – slowly, very slowly!

Eventually, and I really do mean, "eventually", to my immense relief the track widened and leveled out again. There were signs that people had used the track, if not vehicles. Then I saw a small house, and then another. Phew! Now there was a track junction, and this was definitely not on the map. And having driven for so long at such a painfully slow speed, I had to admit that I didn't have an accurate idea where I was, save for the general area. I couldn't even see this hamlet on my old map. Turn left or turn right? My instinct and looking at the stars suggested right, but I wasn't absolutely sure and it was getting late.

As I looked left I saw a building. Built of stone, it looked something like a hall, or maybe even originally a barn, with lights on, a beer sign outside, and I could hear men talking loudly

inside. I slowly reversed the vehicle to the side of the dirt road, and cautiously went and knocked on the door. I had no idea what sort of reception I might get. It was completely dark outside, I was a total stranger, uninvited, and from the sound of things the men were drinking and having a good old time. A rugged looking man answered, stared at me for a second or two, and then with a warm smile welcomed me inside as if it was the most natural thing in the world! My Albanian language skills were quite decent at that time and I had a slight Shkodra accent – well, with the many grammatical mistakes I am sure I frequently made I was perhaps more like an uneducated "malok" than a cultured "Shkodrani"! I introduced myself and explained my predicament and what had happened. By that time the men had all gathered around me and were laughing and slapping me on the back and I heard "he crossed that old bridge and drove down that unused track" more than once! They insisted that I shared their food and had a drink with them all. I asked if I could bring Estella inside and they said of course (there were no other women there). I couldn't help but wonder what they were thinking about having this strange Brit who spoke passable Albanian, with an oriental woman, in their small gathering place! I have said it so many times already – the hospitality was incredible, and I feel ashamed that I cannot even remember the name of this small place. In the unlikely event that someone from there somehow stumbles upon this little book, please forgive me, and do contact me and let me know where I was! I can imagine you, dear reader, thinking "well, that is highly unlikely". Well, let me tell you something……..
We had been sitting there for a while, drinking, eating and chatting when suddenly there was another slap on my back, and in perfect London-English a voice said,

"Hi mate. What are you doing here?"

WHAT? I swung around to see this beaming face grinning ear to ear. He explained that he was indeed from this small place, but that he had lived in England for some time and was just back visiting. More chat, more laughter, more drink and food, and then I said that it was getting late and I really needed to get back to Tirana. The English-speaking chap said firmly that it was far too dark and late and it would be better if we stayed at his house overnight. I was all ready to accept – afterall, I had already broken every rule in my diplomatic training about caution, where I went, hours of darkness, always making sure someone knew where I was, and so on, so why not stay overnight? I looked at Estella and she vehemently shook her head – we had to get back. I explained that we had no overnight things and, particularly for Estella, we had to go. He tried to insist, saying that his wife was home and she could give everything a visiting woman might need. Sadly, I knew that we should go, and so we did, but to be honest, I was disappointed – I would love to have stayed! And should this modest tome somehow fall into your hands, Albanian-Londoner, I apologise again for forgetting names but your warm welcome and offers of hospitality will never be forgotten!

The rest of the journey was uneventful. In fact, we were back on the main road within 10 or 15 minutes and heading back down to Tirana and home.

Despite my embarrassing lapses of memory in telling this story, it was again such a beautiful reminder of the wonderful traditions of the Albanian people that it has remained so clearly in my mind and had to be told.

A COLLECTION OF OLD MAGAZINE ILLUSTRATIONS ABOUT ALBANIA

All those years ago, can it really be so long, after I was selected to become the British Defence Attaché in Albania, I quickly became fascinated by Albanian history and culture as I hope this book has already made crystal clear. I threw myself wholeheartedly into learning the language as best I could, ably helped by my three excellent teachers, Edlira Babamusta-Gay, Blerina Piho and Endrit Shijaku. I had new skills to learn, more courses to attend, and yet somehow this wasn't enough for me. I started to read as much as I possibly could about this country which was quickly to snatch my heart, immersing myself completely into its fascinating history and culture. A little piece of me is still in Albania all this time later.

I find myself wishing to write about books I have read about the country, about more wonderful Albanians I met, and conversations enjoyed, but I must not digress in this short chapter as I wish this to focus on something more specific.

Still in London today, if one knows where to look, one may find many almost unbelievably old-fashioned little shops tucked away seemingly unchanged in a hundred years, and yet somehow still managing to survive by selling a specific niche product, be it handmade umbrellas, old fashioned shaving accoutrements, hats, antique books, maps, old prints – whatever one is searching for. I was aware of one such store which sold lithographic prints, carefully removed from old English magazines. I decided to visit one day after yet another challenging couple of hours of trying to get my head around some complicated Albanian grammatical rule and avoiding being slapped by Blerina's ruler for failing in some conjugation (Blerina denies ever having hit me, but I assure you she did! Have I mentioned that already? (But she was a great teacher as were Edlira and Endrit)). The old store seemed to be as old as the prints it sold. Tucked away in a narrow alleyway behind one of the theatres, and coincidentally just a few yards from "Kafe Koha" – an Albanian café/bar/restaurant where Endrit and I would sometimes visit after, or occasionally during, a lesson. I wondered if I could find an old map of Albania perhaps, thinking it might be an interesting decoration for my wall when I moved to Albania.

The closest I could find was a nicely illustrated map from the latter half of the 19th century entitled "*The Turkish Empire in Europe*", which I bought. Whilst browsing, the owner of the shop pulled out a large print from 1880 called "*Sketches in Albania: A Meeting of the Albanian League*" that had been hand-tinted, and which when mounted and framed would be a nice size and interesting picture. I had to buy that too.

Little did I realize that those two purchases would be the start of a collection of old magazine lithographs which continues to grow until today. I've not counted how many I have bought. Certainly they cover two and a half walls in the sitting room in my studio from waist level to ceiling, with hardly a gap between them. I guess I must have 60 or so in my collection now, most of which are framed in simple black wooden frames, nicely mounted, and hanging on my walls in what has become my 'Albania Room', full of my prints, books about Albania, my çifteli, three old jeleke (waistcoats) I somehow collected, and even an old wooden crib bought in Kruja. I often sit with my coffee in this room and simply relax, looking at all these fascinating scenes. Occasionally I attempt to play my çifteli (regretting never having learnt properly) and I cannot help staring at one large print from 1889 which shows a group of men sitting around playing çiftelis and lutes, whilst others dance merrily around them. I keep telling myself that one day I will find someone to teach me properly – or is that another fantastical "dream" such as I used to share with my old friend Riza Lahi?

Part of the author's collection of antique magazine illustrations.

Most of these prints are from the 1880s, but with a few older ones dating back to the 1850s, and I have allowed myself to include one or two from the Second World War period. Most are from the period 1880-95. I've included a few maps because they also help tell the story and it is fascinating to see the changing borders over time. I wish I had the articles which must have accompanied the pictures, but I guess most collectors are only interested in the actual pictures rather than the text, and consequently, regrettably, it is very rare for the pictures to be bought with the related article.

With a few exceptions, the majority of the prints are from *"The Illustrated London News"*. This English magazine was first published on the 14th May 1842 and was the first illustrated weekly news magazine in the world. It was founded by a chap called Herbert Ingram who, coincidently, was born in Boston in Lincolnshire, England which is just a few miles up the road from where my parents last lived, and close to where my sister, Louise, still does. There is a statue of Ingram in Boston's market square. When I took my first appointment as a young officer in Hong Kong in 1980 this lovely magazine was still in print, and I recall one

ALBANIAN WAR-DANCE IN THE CAMP NEAR DULCIGNO, DURING THE FEAST OF THE RAMAZAN.
DRAWN ON THE SPOT BY OUR SPECIAL ARTIST, R. C. WOODVILLE.—SEE PAGE 337.

charming English lady (who was in fact one of the most senior female army officers at that time, and who had somewhat taken this very young and fresh-faced officer under her motherly wing) advising me to subscribe so as not to lose all contact with home! Little did she, or I, know that many years later *"The Illustrated London News"* would be my greatest pleasure not of news from England but rather for antique copies providing me with prints of Albania!

One of the later prints in the author's collection, most are considerably older than this.

There have been a number of foreign artists who painted or sketched in Albania. Perhaps the most famous was Edward Lear who toured the country in 1848. But the vast majority of my prints were drawn by an artist called Richard Caton Woodville

(1856 – 1927). Sometimes he signed his work "R.C. Woodville" and often "R. Caton Woodville". Born in England, Woodville Junior was the son of Richard Caton Woodville Senior who was also a talented American artist. 'Our' Woodville became most well-known for his paintings of British battle scenes of the late 19th and early 20th centuries. He studied at the Düsseldorf School of Painting, and then briefly in Russia before moving to Paris to study under the famous Jean-Léon Gérôme. His work featured in a number of magazines during his lifetime, including *"The Tatler"*, *"Strand Magazine"* and *"Cornhill Magazine"*, but he spent most of his career working for *"The Illustrated London News"*.

Woodville experienced numerous battles first-hand including the 1877-78 Russo-Turkish War and the 1882 Anglo-Egyptian War, both of which he painted and drew. He also painted scenes from the Second Anglo-Afghan War, Zulu War, and the First Boer War, Second Boer War and the First World War. *"The Illustrated London News"* also commissioned him to paint a number of historical battles.

He wrote a book called *"Random Recollections"* which was published in London in 1914. I have an e-copy but would love to find an original. He devotes a complete chapter of the book to his time in Albania at the end of the Russo-Turkish war. Later in the book he espouses the great hunting he also enjoyed in Albania, but as I am a vegetarian, I will skip over that! He clearly loved his adventures in Albania and that attracts him to me even more. Understandably the book is written in somewhat quaint period language, and with the somewhat typical English understated style of expression, so when reading it one needs to do so with that period and style in mind:-

> *"My great friends at this time were two Albanian Beys both wealthy landowners. One bore the name of Betchi Churcha, which means the lamb, and to prove his lamb-like nature he had already forty-five murders to his account. The last one he had committed only a few days before my return to*

Scutari. He had a row with a man over a game of billiards, and then took himself off and waited his chance. When his opponent appeared, he shot him in the back."

He continued:

"Another great friend of mine was one Nik Lekha, one of the principal chiefs of the Clementi tribe. This gentleman, when taking a stroll through the bazaar, was accosted by a shop-keeper for an unpaid bill, and the bill not being settled, he called Nik Lekha, who was a Roman Catholic..... Nik immediately drew his yatagan, collared the shopkeeper by his back hair, by which Mohammed might have carried him up to Paradise, and calmly sabred his head off. He then made a bolt for it, running through the bazaar with the bloody trophy in his hand. There was at once a wild cry, Mohammedans ran together, whilst there followed a wild fusillade, lasting about half an hour, between the two parties."

Reading the full account one clearly has the impression that he genuinely enjoyed and cherished these colourful friendships. There is another story in the book which made me smile, partly because of the way Woodville tells it, and partly because it reminds me of those great Albanian traditions of hospitality and protecting one's guests:

"After a ride of some twenty miles, we had arrived at the Khan of Koplick, where we were just having refreshments and coffee, when four awful-looking Bosniak ruffians came in and sat themselves down, unfortunately between us and our firearms, which were hanging on the wall behind them. These men then told my monk that they had been ordered to bring my head to Gusigne, so things began to look jolly awkward for me, not to say unpleasant. He then explained, and told them he was surprised they should be so inhospitable after having accepted my coffee; but argument did not seem to prevail. Luckily for me, at the

It reminded me of two lines in the Kanun of Leka Dukagjini:

"If you accompany your guest in his way, you are responsible for any dishonor that someone may cause him."

"Si t'i prish mikut, çdo dhûnë t'I bajë kuej ky, lypet mbë ty."

And

"Do not accompany your guest on his way; or, if you do accompany him, you must keep your eyes open, lest someone dishonor him or treat him badly."

"Mikit mos I prij, a, 'si t'I prijshë, do të hapish syt qi mos t'I bajë kuej ndo'i dhunë a punë të ligë."

I could go on, but perhaps I have said sufficient to put this collection of prints into some sort of context.

1880 print in the author's collection:
"The Albanian question: Tusi offered in exchange for Gusinje."

Some of Woodville's pictures in my collection include:

- *"Demonstration on the Adriatic Coast: Albanians from Scutari Crossing the Boyana to Occupy Dulcigno"*, dated 1880.

- *"Life in Albania: Gipsy Girls Fishing"*, dated 1893.

- *"The Revolt in Albania – Sketch at a Turkish Frontier Post"*, dated 1885.

- *"Her Lord and Master – A Scene in a North Albania House"*, dated 1895.

- *"On the Castle at Scutari, Albania"*, dated 1883.

- *"Albania Sketches: Retribution – The End of a Blood Feud"*, dated 1880.

And my favourite because it was on the cover of the 2nd October, 1880, Illustrated London News:

- *"Albanian War Dance in the Camp near Dulcigno, During the Feast of Ramazan."*

Tragically, on the 17th August 1927, Woodville was found dead in his studio in London, shot by a revolver which was also found at the scene. An inquest determined that he was of unsound mind and had committed suicide. As has happened to far too many artists throughout history, and despite his earlier fine reputation, he was effectively destitute at the time of his death. His grave, in St Mary's Catholic Cemetery in Harrow Road adjacent to Kensal Green cemetery, was not marked until September 2013 when a headstone, commissioned by his great-grandson, was placed on the grave. Next time I am in London I will visit and pay my respects. He may be amused to know that a century later prints of his excellent drawings of Albania are being enjoyed by me on the other side of the world!

A print from 1880 in the author's collection:
"Demonstration on the Adriatic Coast: Albanians from Scutari cross the Boyana
to occupy Dulcigno."

Collecting these prints has given me much pleasure and I often look at them and wonder at the stories behind them. I have already mentioned in another short chapter that some years ago my old friend, poet and author, Zoti Riza Lahi and I tentatively discussed an idea to have an exhibition of the prints alongside some of his poems. With hindsight I am now not quite sure how that would have gone together, but the idea was nice!

Oftentimes I have thought that I must draw a line and not purchase any more prints, especially as I have effectively run out of space to exhibit more on my walls. I am also concerned that they will deteriorate especially in the humidity of the Far East where I live, which would be extremely sad as I believe that together as a single collection they are a wonderful and perhaps unique visual record of Albania at that period in history. Yet time and time again I will come across another print which I don't have in the collection and can't resist purchasing "just one more"!

At the time of writing I have five in my friendly neighbourhood framing shop – I need to make some more wall space!

MIGJENI
(13th October 1911 – 26th August 1938)

Why am I including a short essay on the poet and writer, Migjeni, rather than one of many others. I could write about Naim Frashëri, Fan Noli, Ernest Koliqi, Gjergj Fishta or any one of a host of others. Interestingly in my 1955 copy of Stuart Mann's book, "Albanian Literature", which claimed to be the very first outline of Albanian literature in English, he donated only 5 sentences to Migjeni, and those in his section "Novel" and not a single example of his in the "Poetry" part of the book. In contrast, in Robert Elsie's excellent 2015 book, "Classical Albanian Literature – A Reader" he was much more generous, allotting 35 pages – more than for any other writer.

I have decided to include Migjeni in this small book because of his importance not to the stirring of nationalism but to the development of contemporary Albanian writing. Gjergj Fishta and other writers from Shkodra had been the mainstream of writers in the country up until the early 1930s and their contribution to the development of sophistication in Albanian literature should not be taken lightly, but still their style was somewhat traditional. It was, however, Migjeni and Poradeci who modernised ideas in literature in Albania. What makes Migjeni's story even more incredible, however, is that he was only 26 years old when tuberculosis claimed his life before his true potential had time to reach full maturity. What an inspiring figure therefore, to be recognized as one of the key writers in modern Albanian poetry, and yet to have died so young, and without ever having successfully published a single book in his own lifetime.

"Migjeni" was in fact a pen name. His real name was Millosh Gjergj Nikolla, and "Migjeni" was taken from the first two letters of each of his real names, <u>Mi</u>llosh <u>Gj</u>ergj <u>Ni</u>kolla.

Millosh was born in Shkodra. His father, Gjergj Nikolla (1872-1924), came from Dibra, and married Millosh's mother, Sofia

Kokoshi, in 1900. Both were well respected members of the Shkodra community. Millosh attended a Serbian Orthodox elementary school in Shkodra, and then from 1923 to 1925 a secondary school in Bar across the border in Montenegro. Subsequently, in 1925 the 14 year old boy was granted a scholarship to attend a secondary school in Monastir (later called Bitola) in Macedonia, near the Greek border. Monastir had students from Macedonia, Serbia, Turkey and Greece, as well as Albania. Here he studied Old Church Slavonic, Russian, Greek, Latin and French. One can only presume that this international exposure helped to broadly develop the young mind and to expose him to new ideas and concepts.

During the first Balkan War, the Battle of Monastir had taken place in November 1912, just 13 years before Millosh's arrival. It was a battle of pivotal importance, seeing the end of five centuries of Ottoman rule in Macedonia. Whether or not this had any effect on him is a matter of conjecture, but having occurred so recently before his time there, it would be surprising if its effects weren't somehow still felt by his teachers and others with whom he may have come into contact.

He graduated from the school in Monastir in 1927 and entered the Orthodox Seminary of St. John the Theologian, also in Monastir. By this time Millosh's health was already problematic, but he continued his studies at the Seminary for five years, considerably longer than he had spent in either of the two previous places of learning. He was known to be an avid reader of Russian, Serbian and French literature in particular, and became familiar with Dostoyevsky, Tolstoy, and Gorky, as well as authors from the west such as Rousseau, Schiller, Stendhal and Zola. It is said that he spent much more time reading such literature than he did on his scriptural studies, but presumably the Seminary had, at least, annual examinations which would need to be passed in order for one to remain there. If this presumption is correct, suggestions that he virtually ignored the religious studies would seem questionable.

In 1932 he returned to Shkodra after failing to win a scholarship to study in western Europe. Rather than joining the priesthood, the following year he accepted an appointment as an Albanian language teacher at the Serbian village of Vrakë, seven kilometers from Shkodra. It was at this time that the first of his prose and verse are known to have been written, often expressing the anguish of an intellectual grappling within that time and place. In May 1934 his first short prose, *Sokrat i vuejtun a po derr i kënaqun* ("Suffering Socrates or the Satisfied Pig"), was published in the periodical *Illyria*, under his new pen name, Migjeni.

Sadly however, just over a year later, in the summer of 1935, he became seriously ill with tuberculosis, which was to reoccur throughout the remainder of his short life. In the hope of a change in climate and possibly receiving treatment, he travelled to Athens in the July, but returned to Shkodra a month later with no improvement. In the autumn of 1935, he transferred to a school in Shkodra. *Illyria* began publishing his first poems at this time.

On the 12th January 1936 Migjeni wrote to the Tirana based translator, Skënder Luarasi, announcing, "I am about to send my songs to press. Since, while you were here, you promised that you would take charge of speaking to some publisher, '*Gutemberg*' for instance, I would now like to remind you of this promise, informing you that I am ready."

Migjeni applied for another transfer, this time to the mountain village of Puka in north-central Albania, where the air would be fresher, and on 18 April 1936, at the age of 25, he became the headmaster of the somewhat dilapidated school there. Many children attended school barefoot and hungry, and contagious diseases were all too frequent. In the same year his slender volume of 35 poems entitled *Vargjet e Lira* ("Free Verse") was printed by *Gutenberg Press Publisher* in Tirana in 1936, only to be banned by government censorship. The school is now somewhat a tourist attraction as a result of Migjeni having worked there, but within just eighteen months, the surrounding poverty, harsh mountain conditions, and his own ill health resulted in him resigning and seeking medical treatment in Turin. This Italian city was the obvious choice because it was where his sister, Ollga, was studying.

Leaving Shkodra on the 20th December 1937 he arrived in Turin four days later. He hoped that after being cured of his tuberculosis he would be able to study at the Faculty of Arts in the city.

This contagious disease was not rare at this time. In 1918 in France, as an example, 1 in 6 deaths came from TB. During the previous century this tragic figure was at times 50% of all deaths. The pasteurization of milk in the first decades of the 20th century greatly reduced occurrences, but for those infected the only option was usually spending time in a sanatorium. Even so, one statistic from 1916 stated that 50% of those who entered a sanatorium died within 5 years. It was not until 1946 that the development of the antibiotic streptomycin made effective treatment and cure of TB a reality – too late for Migjeni who entered the San Luigi sanatorium in early 1938, and after five months was transferred to the Waldensian hospital in Torre Pellice. Tragically he died on the 26 August 1938, aged just 26.

He wrote at least 24 short prose sketches, ranging from one to five pages in length, which were published between 1933 and 1938 in various periodicals. His impact as a poet, however, is much more widely accepted, even though not voluminous. His short life and frequent ill health resulted in his literary output not to be great in quantity, but it is generally acknowledged to have played a very significant role in the development of modern Albanian writing.

To add balance, it should be mentioned that Migjeni is not without his critics, especially with regards to his prose. One American-Albanian critic has written that he was a Slav and spoke poor Albanian and always spoke Serbo-Croatian at home.

This has been vehemently denied by his family members, stating that they only ever spoke Albanian at home, and he was absolutely Albanian. His grandfather was one of the signatories of the congress for the establishment of the Orthodox Church of Albania in 1922, and his mother (who died in 1916) was a native of Kavajë. Angjelina Ceka Luarasi, daughter of Migjeni's younger sister Ollga, wrote clearly in her book *Migjeni–Vepra*, co-authored with Skënder Luarasi, that Migjeni was of Albanian and certainly not of any Slavic origin. She added that Albanian was his mother tongue and only later did he learn to speak Serbo-Croat. Furthemore, she writes, the family is descended from the Nikolla family from Debar in the Albanian region of Upper Reka (*Reka e Epërme*) in northern Macedonia, and the Kokoshi family. Angjelina maintained that the family used many Slavic names because of their Orthodox faith. His initial profession as an Albanian language teacher and then headmaster would also add doubt to this assertion.

At least one respected academic has commented that his work is littered with spelling mistakes and some grammatical errors. I cannot add any expert opinion as I have not seen his works in their original writing, but strongly feel one must compare his written work to other contemporaries, and if indeed his spelling is considerably worse then the criticism is fair, but if not we must see it as not atypical of that period. I feel, in Migjeni's defence, that a slide onto another tangent is justifiable before we sit in our cozy armchairs and criticize, so please indulge me.

The Development of Written Albanian

According to the late, great Albanologist Robert Elsie (with whom I exchanged a number of emails):

> *The hundred years between 1750 and 1850 were an age of astounding orthographic diversity in Albania. In this period, the Albanian language was put to writing in at least ten different alphabets – most certainly a record for European languages ... the diverse forms in which this old*

Writers from the north, influenced by the Catholic Church, used Latin letters, those in southern Albania and under the influence of the Greek Orthodox church used Greek letters, while others throughout Albania and under the influence of the Turks used Arabic letters. There were some attempts to standardize a written form of Albanian between 1750 and 1850, and the thirst for written Albanian was seen as an important, if not essential, element of national identity.

The first school known to teach Albanian was a Franciscan school in Shkoder, in 1855.

Miranda Vickers wrote in her excellent book, "The Albanians, A Modern History",

Whilst many Albanians profited under Ottoman rule, their cultural advancement was severely restricted. Nowhere was the Albanian language taught, nor had a standard alphabet been devised. Books In Albanian were virtually non-existent, and what few schools there were taught only in Turkish, Greek, or Italian. In contrast to the tolerance shown to other nationalities, the Ottoman administration opposed the use of the Albanian language in schools so as to delay the awakening of an Albanian national consciousness."

There were attempts to form groups to revive the Albanian language, such as the "Albanian Cultural Association" in Bucharest in 1850, "Albanian Committee" in Istanbul, formed in 1877. It wasn't long before the Ottomans had had enough however, and the Albanian language was banned from being taught in schools, and Moslem families were forced to remove their children from the Albanian managed schools. The Orthodox were no better, threatening parents with ex-communication if they did not remove their children from Albanian schools. Secret societies were formed to teach this rich, beautiful and ancient language, but when discovered these were closed down by both Ottomans as well as the Greek Orthodox clergy.

The issue of standardizing a written form of the language was discussed in the League of Prizren in 1878, but it was not until the Congress of Manastir, in November 1908, that agreement was reached that the Latin alphabet should be used, with the addition of twelve more letters.

Edith Durham describes this in some detail in some of her books, and let's not forget that she traveling in Albania during the period of Migjeni's life. Here is one such quotation from her book, "20 years of Balkan Tangle", the context is that she is discussing the fallout of the Treaty of Berlin, which unfairly took away Albanian lands from the country and how, as a result, the Albanians rose in force:

> ......*that caused the formation of the Albanian League, and a national uprising by means of which the Albanians retained some of the said lands in spite of the Powers. This induced Abdul Hamid [he 34th Sultan of the Ottoman Empire] for a short time to relax the ban upon the Albanian language. At once, national schools were opened, and books and papers, came from Albanian presses. The Sultan, alarmed by the rapid success of the national movement, again prohibited the language. Schoolmasters were condemned to long terms of imprisonment. As much as 15 years was the sentence that could be, and was, inflicted upon anyone found in possession of an Albanian paper, and the Greek priests entered enthusiastically into the persecution. But Albanian was not killed, leaders of the*

She goes on to tell how, even when she was in the country, New Testaments written in Albanian had to be smuggled in, and were eagerly sought after by Albanian Catholic, Orthodox and Moslem alike, as they were the only source of reading the Albanian language.

Back to Migjeni

Yes, dear reader, a standardized alphabet for Albanian was not agreed until 1908, just three years before Migjeni was born. Now of course this situation was rapidly changing during his short life, thankfully, but with this perspective is it not unfair to sit in our armchairs and criticize if his spelling and grammar were not perfect? I do not claim to be a great scholar, but I strongly feel we must always put things in the context of time and place.

His tragically short life makes it nigh on impossible to fully assess his potential. It would be understandable in one so young that not all his works were mature, perhaps especially some of his prose. One may attempt to add labels and categorise Migjeni as a product of the Zogist era, or (as some communists did) suggest he was the precursor of socialist-realism in literature (whilst at the same time refusing to accept some of his subject matter). One can only hypothetically wonder how persecuted he might have been, or how constrained his writing would have become, had he lived into the communist era. So many writers and artists were persecuted during those dark decades if they didn't do as the State demanded.

The bottom line however, whether one wishes to pick holes and criticize, unfairly in my opinion, or attempt to stick labels on him, is that beyond doubt, as is widely recognized, Migjeni was one of the most influential writers in the development of modern Albanian literature, not only in his style of writing, but especially in the subject matter which was far removed from the folklore, nationalism and romanticism of life which authors preceding him tended towards.

Here are a couple of examples of his wonderful poetry.

Poem of poverty

Poverty, brothers, is a mouthful that's hard to swallow,
A bite that sticks in your throat and leaves you in sorrow,
When you watch the pale faces and rheumy eyes
Observing you like ghosts and holding out thin hands;
Behind you they lie, stretched out
Their whole lives through, until the moment of death.
Above them in the air, as if in disdain,
Crosses and stony minarets pierce the sky,
Prophets and saints in many colours radiate splendour.
And poverty feels betrayed.

Poverty carries its own vile imprint,
It is hideous, repulsive, disgusting.
The brow that bears it, the eyes that express it,
The lips that try in vain to hide it
Are the offspring of ignorance, the victims of disdain,
The filthy scraps flung from the table
At which for centuries
Some pitiless, insatiable dog has fed.
Poverty has no good fortune, only rags,
The tattered banners of a hope
Shattered by broken promises.

Poverty wallows in debauchery.
In dark corners, together with dogs, rats, cats,
On mouldy, stinking, filthy mattresses,

Naked breasts exposed, sallow dirty bodies,
With feelings overwhelmed by bestial desire,
They bite, devour, suck, kiss the sullied lips,
And in unbridled lust the thirst is quenched,
The craving stilled, and self-consciousness lost.
Here is the source of the imbeciles, the servants and the beggars
Who will tomorrow be born to fill the streets.

Poverty shines in the eyes of the newborn,
Flickers like the pale flame of a candle
Under a ceiling blackened with smoke and spider webs,
Where human shadows tremble on damp stained walls,
Where the ailing infant wails like a banshee
To suck the dry breasts of its wretched mother
Who, pregnant again, curses god and the devil,
Curses the heavy burden of her unborn child.
Her baby does not laugh, it only wastes away,
Unwanted by its mother, who curses it, too.
How sorrowful is the cradle of the poor
Where a child is rocked with tears and sighs.

Poverty's child is raised in the shadows
Of great mansions, too high for imploring voices to reach
To disturb the peace and quiet of the lords
Sleeping in blissful beds beside their ladies.

Poverty matures a child before its time,
Teaches it to dodge the threatening fist,
The hand which clutches its throat in dreams,
When the delirium of starvation begins
And when death casts its shadow on childish faces,
Instead of a smile a hideous grimace.
While the fate of a fruit is to ripen and fall,
The child is interred not maturing at all.

Poverty labours and toils by day and night,
Chest and forehead drenched in sweat,

Up to the knees in mud and slime,
And still the empty guts writhe in hunger.
Starvation wages! For such a daily ordeal,
A mere three or four leks and an 'On your way.'

Poverty sometimes paints its face,
Swollen lips scarlet, hollow cheeks rouged,
And body a chattel in a filthy trade.
For service in bed for which it is paid
With a few lousy francs,
Stained sheets, stained face and stained conscience.

Poverty leaves a heritage as well,
Not cash in the bank or property you can sell,
But distorted bones and pains in the chest,
Perhaps leaves the memory of a bygone day
When the roof of the house, weakened by decay,
By age and the weather collapsed and fell,
And above all the din rose a terrible cry
Cursing and imploring, as from the depths of hell,
The voice of a man crushed by a beam.
Under the heel, says the priest, of a god irate
Ends thus the life of a dissolute ingrate.
And so the memory of such misfortunes
Fills the cup of bitterness passed to generations.

Poverty in drink seeks consolation,
In filthy taverns, with dirty, littered tables,
The thirsting soul pours glass after glass
Down the throat to forget its many worries,
The dulling glass, the glass satanic,
Caressing with a venomous bite.
And when, like grain under the scythe, the man falls
To the floor, he giggles and sobs, a tragicomic clown,
And all his sorrow in drink he drowns
When one by one, a hundred glasses downs.

Poverty sets desires ablaze like stars in the night
And turns them to ashes, like trees struck by lightning.

Poverty knows no joy, but only pain,
Pain reducing you to such despair
That you seize the rope and hang yourself,
Or become a poor victim of 'paragraphs.'

Poverty wants no pity, only justice!
Pity? Bastard daughter of cunning fathers,
Who like the Pharisees, beating the drum
Ostentatiously for their own sly ends,
Drop a penny in the beggar's hands.

Poverty is an indelible stain
On the brow of humanity through the ages.
And never can this stain be effaced
By doctrines decaying in temples.

[*Poema e mjerimit*, from the volume *Vargjet e lira*, Tirana: Ismail Mal' Osmani 1944, translated from the Albanian by Robert Elsie, published in English in *Migjeni, Free Verse*, Peja: Dukagjini 2001, p. 34-43]

Suffering

For some time now
I have seen clearly
How from suffering my eyes are growing larger,
The furrows in my face and brow are growing deeper,
And my smile has grown bitter...
...and I have come to realize
That the coming days
Will no longer be constructive ones
Of energy and work, but simply the passing
Of a waning life.

With time, I have come to see
How this treacherous life
Has singed
Each of my senses,
One by one,
Until nothing remains
Of the joy
I once had.

Oh life,
I did not know before
How much I dreaded
Your grip
That strangles
Ruthless.

But helpless now,
I gaze into the mirror and see
How from suffering my eyes are growing larger,
The furrows in my face and brow are growing deeper,
And that soon I will become
A tattered banner,
Worn and torn
In the battles of life.

[*Vuejtja*, from the volume *Vargjet e lira*, Tirana: Ismail Mal'
Osmani 1944, translated from the Albanian by Robert Elsie,
published in English in *Migjeni, Free Verse*, Peja: Dukagjini 2001,
p. 123]

COLOURFUL KRUJA

As mentioned in the chapter "First Encounters with Albania", one of the first road direction signs I noticed on my very first day in Albania was that of Kruja, some 20 kilometers north of Tirana. It was to become a regular trip, such a fascinating place and so close to the capital city. It is always on the itinerary of tourists and visitors and I was to escort various guests to Kruja over the next three years, and on two occasions attended wedding functions there. I always enjoyed the winding road up the hill to an altitude of 600 metres to the foot of Mount Krujē (Mali i Krujës) where the town itself is located. From various vantage points one may look behind to the mountain behind, and forward across the plain of the Ishëm River.

Kruje had been inhabited by the ancient Illyrian tribe of the Albani from whom the modern name, Albanians, derives. Some believe Kruja was the site of Albanopolis, the main centre of this tribe, whist others believe it to be close by, near the Iron Age site of Zgerdhesh. The town has a very rich history indeed, the details of which deserve a book to themselves, so please excuse me dear reader for doing no more than skating over them and mentioning but a few highlights.

During the Illyrian Wars, the first of which started in 229BC, the town was captured by the Roman Republic.

Jump forward 1400 years, forgive me, and in 1190 Kruja became the capital of the first Albanian state, the Principality of Arbanon, or Arber. The Albanian principalities were created in the Middle Ages as territories ruled over by Albanian clan leaders, and Arbanon was the first.

These principalities grew in power over the next couple of hundred years, but remained fractured, all too often fighting each other and blind to the threat of the invading Ottomans in the latter part of the 14th century who took advantage of the situation in the territory. In the early 15th century, the Ottomans captured Kruja, but in November 1443 the great national hero Gjergj Kastrioti, better known as Skanderbeg, recaptured the town.

The following year some of the principalities united under the military and diplomatic alliance called the League of Lezhe (*Lidhja e Lezhës*), often called the Albanian League *(Lidhja Arbërore)*, which was signed on the 2nd March 1444, thus forming what is usually acknowledged as the first unified and independent Albanian country.

"The Kingdom of Albania" (*Mbretëria e Arbërisë)* had previously existed, but this had been established by Charles of Anjou admittedly with the help of the local Albanian nobility. Charles I (1226/27 – 1285) was Count of Provence, Count of Forcalquier in the Holy Roman Empire, Count of Anjou and Maine, King of Sicily, Prince of Achaea and in 1272 proclaimed himself King of Albania. As if all that wasn't enough for one man, in 1277 he purchased a claim to the Kingdom of Jerusalem!

This "Kingdom of Albania" lasted from 1272 until the late 1360s when Karl Topia seized Durrës (the capital city at that time), and other territories, including Kruja, and this period became known as "The Princedom of Albania". The family gradually lost its power however and Karl's son, Gjergji, surrendered Durrës to the Venetians in 1392. Fascinating though the changes of power, decapitations, power struggles and so on may be, it is taking us off on too much of a tangent from Kruja! Suffice to say, arguably this "Kingdom" was hardly "independent", although it is true that Albanian nobility had been intimately involved and held leadership positions.

Anyhow, returning to the Albanian League, Skanderbeg (1405 – 1468) was selected as leader, "Chief of the League of the Albanian people". By this time the Ottomans were in control of much of Albania, including Kruja. Niketa Thopia, younger brother of Gjergj Topia, captured the town in 1403, but after his death in 1415 the town fell once more to the Ottomans.

Skanderbeg was to successfully seize Kruja in 1443 and then defended it victoriously against three Ottoman sieges. During the 'First Siege of Kruja' in 1450, the 1,500 to 2,000 Albanian troops incredibly managed to repel an invading force of 100,000 men of Sultan Murad II! The Ottomans tried again 1466, and once more the following year with an invading force now increased to 150,000 men, but still the town didn't fall. Skanderbeg was to die in 1468, and ten years later, after a siege which lasted over a year, with the Fourth Siege of Kruja, the town fell.

Dear reader, this is not meant to be a detailed history lesson, and this is a particularly complicated period of Albanian history about which even scholars have different viewpoints. The major external influencers were the Serbs, Venetians and Ottomans, and there were often alliances and betrayals, family links and reversals of positions, and strategic posturing for limit periods of time. In my attempts to simplify this and not make it too dull reading, please forgive me if errors have crept in. My intention is to give "a flavour" rather than an academic account, and if you are inspired to read more I would encourage you to read some of the excellent history books listed in the bibliography.

And now once more I must beg your forgiveness as I am going to jump forward to the days of the rise of Balkan nationalism in the Ottoman Empire in the early years of the 20th century, when again Kruja was to feature strongly.

The increase in nationalism was matched by growing discontent against the Ottomans throughout the Balkans. In 1906 the inhabitants of Kruja revolted, which resulted in the Wali of Shkoder, Sali Zeki Pasha sending four battalions of the Ottoman Empire to crush the rebellion. It wasn't until 20th September (as a complete coincidence, I am writing this on the 20th September some 115 years later!) that both sides agreed to negotiate. They met at the Tallabje quarter of the town but in a complete display of treachery Semsi Pasha led Ottoman soldiers to ambush the Albanian representatives, killing 30.

Revolts against the "Young Turks" increased, the first noteworthy one in Albania occurring in 1910. There were more widespread revolts between January and August of 1912, and this became known as the "Albanian Revolt" and ended in the Declaration of Independence of Albania, but again I am straying from Kruja! However, it is worthy of note that the town was one of the battlefields of the conflict between the short-lived Republic of Central Albania, founded by Essad Toptani, and the Principality of Albania. Toptani succeeded in seizing Kruja in 1914, but in June of the same year it was reincorporated by Prenk Bibë Doda into the Principality of Albania. On the 20th December 1914, as the First World War raged in other parts of Europe, local anti-Essadists, led by Abdi Toptani (one of the signatories of the Declaration of Independence, and Mehmet Gjinali, formed the Union of Kruja which was to extend its authority in central Albania.

After the Italian invasion of Albanian at the start of World War II the town became a protectorate of the Kingdom of Italy. Mustafa Merlika-Kruja became the Prime Minister of the regime and formed a gendarmerie of 300 men to defend the town against any rebellion. However, soon thereafter the resistance leader Abaz Kupi (who I have mentioned in the chapter on the British in Albania in World War Two), raised in Kruja one of the first real Albanian resistance groups. I also mentioned Balli Kombëtar in that same chapter – in 1943 they proposed the creation of a provisional resistance government with Kruja as the capital city, but this was rejected by the leadership of the LNÇ. By the end of November 1944 the last German troops in the Kruja areas were defeated and were replaced by the LNÇ.

The religious history of the town and surrounding area is no less colourful, with pagan rituals in ancient times, to the building of the Catholic and Orthodox churches with bishops of both, and the multitude of sometimes complex stories resulting from the Ottoman infiltration. Then came Bektashism, introduced in the early 18th century, with a tekke dedicated to one of their saints,

Sari Saltik, build near the church of Saint Alexander in Kruja. The building of other tekkes followed. If contemporary writings of the mid-18th century are to be believed, the vast majority of the inhabitants associated themselves as Bektashi. I had the privilege of briefly meeting Dede Reshat, the then leader of the faith in Albania, on quite a few occasions. At the age of 22 he had been put in house arrest by the communist regime, from 1957-67. He and Dedebaba Ahmed Myftar were taken and restricted to a small tekke near Drizar, Mallakastra, not far from Fier in south-west Albania. During these ten years, this small tekke served as the Mother Tekke for all baktashis. Then in 1967, when all places of worship were compulsorily closed, Dede Reshat was forced to labour on a state-owned farm, often suffering physical and psychological abuse at the hands of his jailors. It wasn't until 1990 that he was once again free, then aged 55. Many other religious leaders, priests and monks were imprisoned, tortured or killed during the Hoxha regime.

It would be an incomplete account of Kruja, however brief, without mentioning the castle and Skanderbeg Museum. The castle, located 610 metres above sea level, has commanding views across the lowlands all the way to the Adriatic. Excavations in 1978 found material dating back to the 4th to 2nd centuries BC, including a stamp of the head of Athena. They also discovered burials from the late-Roman and early medieval periods. Later excavations have discovered more finds from the 3rd to 2nd centuries BC. Much of the remains date to the 12th to 15th centuries, and from this period a considerable amount of pottery and other items have been found.

Kruja

The Skanderbeg Museum was founded in 1982 and designed by Enver Hoxha's daughter and son-in-law. It is situated within the environs of the castle. To be frank, when I lived in Albania, many of my Albanian friends told me that the museum had been well and truly looted, and most of what could be seen were modern reproductions, and the displays were naïve propaganda in accord with the Hoxha regimes intent. Some of my friends associated it too much with the Hoxha regime which they hated with a vengeance! From reports I have read, however, it is now a much more informative and worthwhile place to visit. Also in Kruja is the National Ethnographic Museum located in the 15 rooms of an Ottoman style house built by Ismail Pashë Toptani in 1764. As I have no personal knowledge of either in recent years, it would be wrong for me to say more. However, I will definitely visit both during my next trip to Albania.

What every visitor to Kruja enjoys is the bazaar. It was restored in the mid 1960s but has managed to retain the atmosphere of an Ottoman-era street. Of architectural note are the extra-long eaves of the buildings which allow water or wet snow to quickly and effectively run off the roofs into the gutters which are built along the centre of the cobbled streets. Inevitably many of the shops contain the typical marble ashtrays in the shape of bunkers, keyrings, postcards and other inexpensive knick-knacks, but there are also shops selling wonderful carpets, handmade artefacts, and genuine antiques.

This fascinating town has such a rich and fascinating history, intertwined with so many important events in the history and development of Albania, that it deserves much more than this short overview can offer. The history is complex and difficult to summarise in so few words, but my aim, as with this whole book, is to leave the reader with an *impression*, not to be a totally reliable source of accurate academic information, although of course I have attempted to be as accurate as possible. It is a place with a character all of its own, and definitely well worthy of a visit and deeper exploration.

The bazaar – Kruja.

ENSNARED BY THE TWO-HEADED EAGLE

As I draw this little book to a close I wish to reflect on why I have become so ensnared by the Albanian "two-headed eagle". In doing so, I will inevitably repeat some things which I have already written about earlier, and I make no excuses for so doing, as it seems a fitting way to end.

I am British and never felt any great affinity to the Balkan area until my first visit to Albania in 2005. I had been in Bosnia very briefly during the war, but had not been involved during the war in Kosovo – the job I was in at the time prevented me deploying there.

In 2003 I had applied to be posted to Nepal. It is a slightly long story which is irrelevant to these tales, so suffice to say there were some unusual and questionable decisions made by those I was not supposed to question. To cut the story very short, I applied and was told I had an excellent chance, but was not selected – surprising as no one else was either. Was the prejudice against mixed marriages which I had directly experienced as a young officer (specifically in certain parts of the army, including the Brigade of Gurkhas) coming back to haunt me again? I had been told that I would never serve with Gurkhas again because of a mixed-race marriage – but surely things must have changed, hadn't they? Strong hints were made to me to apply again three months later, which I did, and to my delight was selected. Three months after that, in fact on the day we were breaking for Christmas, I received a message that I had been de-selected! A few urgent phone calls later and I had ascertained that apparently a (strange) decision had been made that because of the Maoist situation in Nepal, and because my wife was from Taiwan, I could be deemed too attractive a target. Yes, the chap I was taking over from had indeed been kidnapped by the Maoists for a few days, but his wife was English. I consulted with him - he was an expert in the country and saw no reason for me not to be there. Hey ho. I was instructed to fly to our Personnel Centre in Scotland on the first day back to work after the New Year as time was now so short they had to find me a job urgently, and *"be rest assured, we are all on your side."* Why did it not feel like it after all these shenanigans over Nepal?

When I arrived in those offices which could decide the lives of officers and soldiers and their families for the next 2 or 3 years with the flick of a pen, they didn't want to talk about the strange events concerning my de-selection for Nepal, about which I was still extremely unhappy. They did say, however, that they had noted on my file an interest in the Defence Attaché (DA) career field, and suitable recommendations from my bosses. Things were looking up, and with my clearly stated interest in the Indian sub-continent and Asia I had flashes of thoughts of being offered a job as the DA in Thailand, or some other Far Eastern country, or India maybe?

"How about Albania?"

"Albania?"

"Yes, DA Tirana."

"Errrrr....Tirana.....Albania?"

"Yes, but we need an answer within a couple of days if you need to think about it. The Selection Board in January has to allocate you to a job."

"DA in Albania?"

"Yes. Let us know. Otherwise it will probably be another desk job in UK."

"OK, give me a day."

And the interview, deciding the next three (or four if I accepted this proposal as it entailed 12 months' training) years of my life, was over. An hour later I was back at the airport in Glasgow ready to fly back down to London. As I sat waiting for the flight I mulled it all over. It would certainly be an interesting adventure, something different, a new challenge …. Albania ….why not!

I was aware that in agreeing it would, bizarrely, not be a great career move. For further promotion one needed to stay "visible" and "mainstream", and sadly (in my humble opinion) the Ministry of Defence was still grappling over whether one could, or should, be able to enter the DA world as a career stream in which one could be promoted. At that time (I cannot say about today) the answer to that was "no", or at best "highly unlikely". I knew my career was right at the stage where one more well reported year could be the difference between promotion, or not. On the other hand, my personal goal had always been my current rank, Lieutenant Colonel, and I had just spent the last 5 or 6 years in good jobs, done well, done all I was asked to do, and had been well reported on. So did I really want to spend another 3 years behind another desk, a pawn in the game, or did I want to seize the opportunity for something completely different, a life experience rather than a dull desk. In full knowledge that this would involve one year's training which would therefore be a gap in my critically important for promotion annual reports, followed by three years in a job which was far from mainstream and therefore be unseen by most of the career progression influencers, I picked up my mobile phone and called my personnel manager.

"I'm your man for Albania!"

It went before the Board the next week, and they confirmed the plan. I was delighted and excited at a new challenge. When my current post ended I then started nearly a year of preparation, including language training and numerous other courses which are irrelevant to this book.

As mentioned in the opening chapter, part of the training package was an opportunity to spend a month with a family in Albania in order for me to practice my Albanian language and to see something of the country, unofficially, before arriving in diplomatic guise. Before I even got that far however I had started reading everything about the country I could lay my hands on. The more I read, the more fascinated I became. The more I grappled with the complexities of Albanian grammar, the more I wanted to speak it. For inexplicable reasons, unless one believes in past lives (!), within a very short space of time Albania had grabbed my heart and refused to let go. The double-headed eagle's talons were well and truly hooked into me, and I was a willing captive.

The author enjoying the mountain landscape.

I became totally captivated by the varied and awe inspiring landscape, the changing coastline (oh, but please don't lose such beauty for short term gain and lack of planning), the rugged mountains, the hills and valleys. I found that the Eagle could so easily carry my imagination away with it, soaring high into the clouds and becoming lost in thoughts of history and culture and life, raw life. But it wasn't just the natural beauty which made me wish to be part of it, but the people too. As mentioned a few times, I am a vegetarian – a rare thing in Albania, and I am also a Buddhist – perhaps even more unusual! Yet the great and unsurpassed hospitality of the Albanian people made me feel at one with them. Wherever I travelled, and I had the privilege to travel extensively throughout the country, a great effort was always made to make me feel welcome and to provide food which I could eat within the restrictions of my religious beliefs. Unlike in many other parts of the world in which I have lived, I was never once made to feel uncomfortable or like an outsider. I will never ever forget that Albanian hospitality, from those that became close friends to this day, to complete strangers who had never met me before, and probably will never meet me again.

My first real experience was a month living with the two wonderful Shkodrane ladies, Domenika and Justina, whom I have mentioned a few times. Despite my trepidation of being alone, in a city unknown to me, with people never met before, and the only form of communication to be in Albanian of which I was still learning, in no time at all they made me feel completely at home. Their home was spotless, and their garden full of flowers, but it wasn't that, pleasing though it was, it was something more important. I was made to feel part of their family. They treated me like their own nephew and to this day I still feel that I am. As devout Catholics I am not sure what they thought of my Buddhist beliefs, but it was never an obstacle, and I enjoyed visiting their church with them too. Of course I visited them on quite a few occasions over the next few years, but I will always regret that when I left Albania in 2008 I didn't get chance to properly say "farewell". The Gerdeç tragedy occurred which totally consumed my time for the last few weeks and kept me focused in Tirana. Even for myself now looking back, it seems hard to believe that I couldn't find one day, even half a day, to drive to Shkodra once more, but in my heart I know that if I could I would have done. The fact was that I couldn't! I suspect that Domenika and Justina don't realize how much I regret that, nor how much I have continued to feel like part of their family, despite the miles and the years. In fact however, even now, so many years later, I still write to them and send greetings via other friends from Shkodra. I hope they have received at least some of my cards and messages although someone recently told me that nothing I have sent has ever been received – I hope that is not the case.

Shkodra became my favourite area in the whole of Albania, and I have such happy memories of my frequent trips there, and up to Kelmend and Vermosh. But I enjoyed everywhere I went in the country, and this small book is as much about people as it is about the castles, lakes, rivers, mountains and valleys.

I remember the first time I visited Vermosh. I had kindly been invited to join a group of men who were going to spend a night or two up in that beautiful area. I hadn't been in Albania more than a week or two at that time, and on the first hour in Vermosh I made that silly error over money – I confused old lek with new (for those unaware, there is a difference of ten-fold)! We had arrived in Vermosh in the late afternoon, and one of the group had already bought us all lunch en route, and someone else had bought us drinks in Shkodra before we had departed up that gorgeously scenic road which wound its way over the imposing mountains which I always found to be so beautiful. We decided to have some snacks and drinks in the village before proceeding to where we would spend the night.

Keen to be part of the group I quietly sneaked over to the patron to settle the bill. He was very reluctant to let me pay, but eventually I persuaded him to tell me how much it was, which he of course described in old lek, as was the norm. At that time I really had no idea how much things should cost, and as I was trying to pay quietly and quickly my brain didn't calculate how much per head I thought I was being asked for. I therefore quickly counted out my notes and thrust them into his hand before anyone else in the group could stop me. He laughed and quickly explained that I was attempting to pay him ten times too much, pushing most of the notes back into my hand. It would have been so easy to have just said nothing, and in many parts of the world I am sure that it would be seen to be just extra profit from an ignorant foreigner. He didn't. Scrupulously honest, he explained my error, and in that single action received my admiration and trust unforgotten to this day.

The road to Vermosh.

We stayed at the family home of Gjergji Pllumaj and as hosts they could not have been more attentive or welcoming. I have never forgotten that experience and recently sent greetings via someone I met on-line who said they were related to the Pllumaj family. I was to stay with them a few times over the next few years.

The author with zoti Plummaj in Vermosh.

I was fortunate enough to visit Vermosh a further 3 or 4 times, and every time I received nothing but the most amazing hospitality. In order for me to show honesty I should admit that once, returning from Vermosh, a good friend of mine nearly got pushed off the road by some idiot in his large and flashy SUV. Only his driving skills saved him from being pushed over the side of the near-sheer drop. What makes some people behave like that is beyond my understanding – perhaps they have feelings of insecurity and consequently think that if they bully and threaten others, then somehow they will be respected or revered. In my opinion it simply shows their own foolishness, and certainly it has nothing to do with traditional Albanian values. No wonder Lek Dukagjini wrote what he did – it was surely, in part, to prevent such behavior, albeit several hundred years ago and society should have moved forward – unfortunately some people clearly haven't.

Then there were the people I met in Shkodra who were going to amazing lengths in their attempts to improve society for the population as a whole. As I said in my introduction, I have decided not to mention names of people I worked with or who I know to be still working in Albania, but suffice to say, I met some very inspiring people who were working in extremely difficult circumstances.

There was one young man I was fortunate to meet who accompanied us on a couple of visits into the mountains. He was a trained nurse, and it was so obvious that wherever we went he was highly regarded, but not in some sycophantic manner, more of a quiet attitude of great respect. I recall so clearly seeing him on more than one occasion surreptitiously disappearing to assist "behind the scenes" in the preparation of the food when we unexpectedly descended as a group at some place or other. He never said a word, and never let himself be seen, but I silently noted what he was doing, just selflessly wanting to help the host and provide for us, who he considered guests. His actions impressed me so much, and he inspired me greatly.

Kelmend.

But he is but one example and the others know who they are. I have briefly mentioned some in this book. Their attitudes were fine examples to all of us, but perhaps especially for the selfish ones who contribute nothing to society, and are only concerned with self-gain and greed and, through that, holding back true development. Despite their apparent riches those people are worthless compared to those who are quietly working for the greater good.

These are the real "tough and strong" ones – determined to do all they can for others, despite whatever obstacles are put in front of them. They are the ones deserving of respect, not the bullies, the leaches, the criminals, the corrupt. Sadly such people can be found everywhere.

Visiting one of the demining projects in the north in 2007. Those are real brave heroes.

I will restrain myself from straying again into recent world politics and the "post-truth era" we live in, where lies are openly told, and if that is what people wish to believe it is accepted. Isn't this corrupt and criminal behaviour on a large scale when it is instigated by certain national and world leaders? But I guess such people don't care, whatever level of society they may come from! The vast majority of people simply want a better society.

I came to love the people of Albania for their warmth, humour and culture.

A poem by Naim Frasheri comes to mind:

> **The Mind of Man**
> *By Naim Frasheri (1846 – 1900)*
>
> *The road that leads to God's own mind*
> *Is nothing more than of mankind.*
> *If man hold man in high esteem,*
> *He has revered his Maker's name.*
> *Look in our hearts, and He is there;*
> *Our hearts are homes with Him to share.*
> *When God first sought to show his face*
> *He made mankind His dwelling place.*
> *A man that knows his inward mind*
> *Knows what God is. It is mankind.*

I also met many dedicated to the arts - I miss the Opera in Tirana so much. I never had the fortune to meet Irini Qirjako but I managed to see her in concert and I bought a number of her CDs which I still enjoy. Her singing of "Pat y si mundem te jetoj" still sends emotional shivers down my spine. I remember coming down from a beautiful restaurant at the top of Mount Dajti in my car with some friends one day when suddenly I realized that one of the ladies had tears in her eyes and wondered what was wrong, but it was simply the emotion of listening to that song on my car stereo.

Peshkopi.

In Shkodra I used to stop and peer through the window of the artist's studio in the high street near the OSCE offices. Often he was too engrossed in another superb painting to notice me there, but if he saw me we would both smile and pass a brief greeting. In the end I saw one of his paintings of Rozafa Castle painted in a traditional style and I had to buy it. That painting has hung proudly on my living-room wall in Albania, then Nepal, and now here in Taiwan. I hope he would be pleased to hear that.

Whenever I play Djemt e Vjoses rendition of "Margarita" I can't help but to laugh. This was one of the favourite songs of the characterful lady taxi driver, Arsi, mentioned earlier in this book, usually played at high volume with the windows wide open, Arsi would tunefully sing along with gusto! Oh such lovely memories of people and places.

Whilst talking about the arts, I must mention Riza Lahi once more in this summarizing chapter. We became good friends and remained so until sadly he left us a number of years ago. Riza's enthusiasm was infectious and his books and poems wonderful, transforming the reader into different environments, and carrying them along in the stories with ease. With his poems, as with all the best poets, he can describe so much with so few words. He kindly gave me a copy of his book "Vorri Ashikut" which was the first full-length novel I read in Albanian, and which I enjoyed very much indeed, dictionary in hand! I wish my knowledge of the complexities of the Albanian language was good enough to attempt a translation into English, but unfortunately I would only be failing Riza if I tried. As mentioned in the short chapter about him, he once sent me a children's story he had written and asked me to translate it, which I did. I have never forgotten him telling me it was his dream to see it published in English. As mentioned earlier, I am desperately trying to find it again although several changes of computer since then is making it hard to locate. Publishing it in English, with his families permission of course, would be my small way to thank him for his unwavering friendship ..... "Never stop dreaming".

The beautiful cathedral in Korçë.

As I write this, I have Ardit Gjebrea singing his duet with Inva Muja, "Te Dua" playing on my HIFI. What beautiful voices, both.

Then there was the story I have told about my adventure in the road from Millot towards Burrel, and the more interesting return trip! Extraordinary though this might have been anywhere else in the world, it was so typical of the amazing generosity and hospitality of the Albanian people I met on my travels, to be greeted and looked after so well in a small restaurant, miles from anywhere, as if it was the most natural thing and I was a returning old friend instead of being a complete stranger. How many places in the world would that have happened?

There were many others and I am going to break my self-imposed restriction on naming names for just these next two paragraphs. HRH Prince Leka II Zogu and his late father, King Leka I, welcomed me warmly and struck me as wanting nothing but the best for the country and Albanian people. I enjoyed many hours with the King during my three years living there, chatting and reminiscing, and when I told Him the date I was leaving Albania at the end of my tour He insisted that I visited Him last of all after I left my villa en-route for the port of Durres as He wanted to be the last to formally bid me farewell. Of course I did so, and the He gave me a plaque as a memento, and a wonderful letter of appreciation which I treasure to this day. I was then taken by complete surprise when Prince Leka announced that He would escort me to the ferry. Not only that but He even boarded the ferry with me and saw me to my cabin. I suspect my reaction didn't display how much I appreciated this but I was so totally surprised at this amazing gesture, and I was partly thinking of the long drive from Bari in Italy all the way to UK, and in all honesty feeling somewhat emotional about leaving my beloved Albania, and also uncertain about my next three years in Nepal, and, and and.....but I was hugely touched and extremely grateful. I still wear the very special pin which was given to me by the Family – it means a tremendous amount to me.

Sadly because of the events after the Gerdeç tragedy, most of my formal farewells had been in private but I was thrilled when Lieutenant General Luan Hoxha, the Chief of the General Staff, found time to meet and award me with the "Medaljen Për Shërbimet të Vecanta" ("Medal for Special Service"), and a lovely certificate.

He explained that this was the highest medal he could personally award me. Needless to say, these are also personal treasures which mean so much to me. We had been good friends and I respected him greatly.

The author with Lieutenant General Luan Hoxha, the Chief of the General Staff.

I should definitely praise Diella at my favourite restaurant in Ishull i Lezhes and the wonderful welcome and gorgeous food which she and her husband always gave me. I visited so many times. Sometimes I would just turn up, sometimes alone and sometimes with other guests.

Other times I would telephone in advance, but no matter how busy they were, it always felt like yet another home I was returning to. Sometimes after eating I would take her dog for a walk and play on the beach. Such wonderful memories.

If I start to list everyone in closing this small book, there is a danger that I will forget some. Certainly I am missing some key people that I would like to mention – those I met professionally in the Ministry of Defence and also in the Police in Shkodra, but not knowing if they would welcome their names being mentioned or not, I will resist, but they know who they are and I think of them all most warmly. I miss them all, and am extremely happy that I am still in contact with some.

I have many more stories to tell to illustrate the best of the spirit of the Albanian people as far as I witnessed, but perhaps I have already said enough to express the beauty and spirit of those Albanians who continue to cherish the traditional values of their marvelous heritage, at home and abroad.

Rugged beauty.

So let me end as I began: somehow that double-headed eagle has pierced my heart, and although I have now emigrated to Taiwan, part of me will always be in Albania...probably somewhere in the mountains overlooking Shkodra or in that great city itself! As soon as I can travel again, after this dreadful Covid pandemic, I hope to visit once more and I will sit in a café somewhere in Shkodra, probably alongside the lake, and toast my old friend Riza Lahi, wishing he was there too.

The ever so varied landscape that can be found in Albania, for those willing to look, is stunning, north to south. But memories of the Albanian people, with their beautiful and intricate language, their ancient customs and traditions, their unrivalled hospitality and genuine desire to look after their guests, those memories will live with me forever.

*****

An abridged extract from "Tracks of the Seasons"
By Ernest Koliqi (1901 – 75)

To Myself

With what high hopes you left your mother's fond embrace,
And tramped along the ways 'neath many foreign skies,
A dreamy wanderer in many a distant place.
Your life was filled in turn with laughter and with sighs.
But swallow-like, in spring your thoughts returned once more
Back to the former nest, to build it as of old.
You came. A high ideal inside your breast your bore.
A song upon your lips all ready to unfold...
Your brow all garlanded with myrtle and with bay,
You fain would wake the world, shed light on mount and mere...

....

Mark D. Vickers
Taiwan
28th November 2021
(Albania National Day)

ANNEX A

BOOKS BY EDITH DURHAM

Through the Lands of the Serb (1904)
The Burden of the Balkans (1904)
High Albania (1909)
The struggle for Scutari (1914)
Twenty Years of Balkan Tangle (1920)
The Sarajevo Crime (1925)
Some Tribal Origins, Laws and Customs of the Balkans (1928)

Albania and the Albanians: selected articles and letters, 1903–1944, edited by Bejtullah Destani (I.B. Tauris, 2001)

The Blaze in the Balkans; selected writings, 1903–1941 edited by Robert Elsie and Bejtullah D Destani (I.B. Tauris, 2014)

ANNEX B

**A SELECTION OF BOOKS BY ROBERT ELSIE
IN THE ENGLISH LANGUAGE**

- *The Dictionary of Albanian Religion, Mythology and Folk Culture. Hurst & Co Ltd. ISBN 978-1850655701.*
- *Balkan Beauty, Balkan Blood: Modern Albanian Short Stories (Writings from an Unbound Europe). Edited by Robert Elsie. Northwestern University Press. ISBN 0-8101-2336-3.*
- *Albanian Literature: A Short History. I. B. Tauris. ISBN 1-84511-031-5.*
- *Songs of the Frontier Warriors: Kenge Kreshnikesh--Albanian Epic Verse in a Bilingual English-Albanian Edition. Robert Elsie and Janice Mathie-Heck, editors. Bolchazy-Carducci Publishers; Bilingual edition. ISBN 0-86516-412-6.*
- *Historical Dictionary of Kosovo. Historical Dictionaries of Europe. 79. Scarecrow Press. ISBN 978-0-8108-7231-8.*
- *Historical Dictionary of Albania. Historical Dictionaries of Europe. 75. Scarecrow Press. ISBN 978-0-8108-6188-6*
- *Biographical Dictionary of Albanian History. I. B. Tauris. ISBN 978-1-78076-431-3.*
- *The Cham Albanians of Greece: A Documentary History. I. B. Tauris. ISBN 978-1-780760-00-1.*
- *The Balkans Wars: British Consular reports from Macedonia in the Final Years of the Ottoman Empire. I. B. Tauris. ISBN 978-1-780760-76-6.*
- *The Tribes of Albania: History, Society and Culture. I.B.Tauris. ISBN 9780857739322.*
- *The Albanian Bektashi: History and Culture of a Dervish Order in the Balkans. Bloomsbury Publishing. ISBN 9781788315715.*

ANNEX C

BRITISH DEATHS IN ALBANIA IN WORLD WAR TWO

What follows is a list of those British and Commonwealth men killed on Albanian land during operations in Albania in World War Two. As so often in the tragedy of war – it is worth noting the young age of most, now lying in an unmarked mass grave somewhere in the park of Tirana.

*****

SOE CASUALTIES

BUTTON, Serjeant, HAROLD VICTOR, 7948572, 2nd, Royal Tank Regiment, R.A.C., attd. Force 399, Special Operations Executive. Accidentally drowned near Lesh 12 October 1944. Age 21.

CARELESS, Captain, ALFRED, 243988, Royal Armoured Corps. , attd., Special Operations Executive. Killed in an air crash (part of Brig Nicholls party lost whilst being inserted – delivery aircraft hit a mountain near Tukat) 20 October 1943. Age 31.

LAYZELL, Major, GORDON EDWARD, 130712, South Lancashire Regiment, attd., Special Operations Executive. Died at Staravece. 2 February 1944. Age 31.

MARTIN-LEAKE, Major, STEPHEN PHILIP (served as Leake), Intelligence Corps, Attd Special Operations Executive. Died at Sheper, 7th June 1944. Age 38. Buried at Sheper in South Albania.

NICHOLLS, Brigadier, ARTHUR FREDERICK CRANE, G C, E R D, Coldstream Guards. , attd., Special Operations Executive (2 I/C of the British Military Mission in Albania inserted 16th Oct 1943). Died of exposure near Valijas 11 February 1944. Age 33.

ROBERTS, Corporal, SIDNEY GEORGE, 5443791, M M, Durham Light Infantry, attd. Force 133, Special Operations Executive Died of pneumonia at Brace 22 December 1943. Age 29.

ROCKINGHAM, Signalman, DAVID WILLIAM, 2390796, Royal Corps of Signals. , attd., Special Operations Executive. Killed in an air crash (part of Brig Nicholls party lost whilst being inserted – delivery aircraft hit a mountain near Tukat) 20 October 1943. Age 21.

SPILJE RAID CASUALTIES

AVEYARD, Lance Serjeant, HERBERT, 3251200, 2nd Bn., Highland Light Infantry (City of Glasgow Regiment). 29 July 1944. Age 29.

BARR, Private, ALEXANDER, 3326243, 2nd Bn., Highland Light Infantry (City of Glasgow Regiment). 29 July 1944. Age 29.

CASEY, Private, JOHN, 2939334, 2nd Bn., Highland Light Infantry (City of Glasgow Regiment). 29 July 1944. Age 22.

MOORES, Serjeant, JACK ERNEST, 5767479, Royal Norfolk Regiment, and No. 2, Commando 29 July 1944. Age 37.

SENNETT, Lieutenant, ALAN MACDONALD, 176413, 2nd Bn., Highland Light Infantry (City of Glasgow Regiment). 29 July 1944. Age 23.

SWANNEY, Private, NORMAN, 3328173, 2nd Bn., Highland Light Infantry (City of Glasgow Regiment). 29 July 1944. Age 24.

SARANDA RAID CASUALTIES

BAIN, Sergeant Major, JAMES SIDNEY, PLY/X746, No. 40 R.M. Commando., Royal Marines. 9 October 1944. Age 32.

BANTING, Chaplain 4th Class, The Rev. GARETH BERNARD, 159706, Royal Army Chaplains' Department, attd. No.2, Commando 10 October 1944. Age 32.

CLARKE, Gunner, ALFRED JOHN DOUGLAS, 902982, Royal Artillery, and No. 2, Commando 9 October 1944. Age 23.

COYLE, Lieutenant, JAMES ALBERT, 255387, Royal Artillery, and No. 2, Commando 9 October 1944.

GEE, Corporal, HAROLD, 3864592, The Loyal Regiment (North Lancashire), and No. 2, Commando 10 October 1944. Age 24.

HILES, Captain, WILLIAM JENKIN, No. 40 R.M. Commando, Royal Marines. 9 October 1944.

MACPHERSON, Captain, MICHAEL STUART, No. 40 R.M. Commando, Royal Marines. 9 October 1944.

PARSONS, Captain, GEORGE ALEXANDER, 162020, M C, Somerset Light Infantry, and No. 2, Commando. 9 October 1944. Age 23.

PINCHER, Marine, RONALD, PLY/X113394, No. 40 R.M. Commando, Royal Marines. 10 October 1944. Age 19.

PRATT, Marine, GEORGE STEPHEN, CH/X3203, No. 40 R.M. Commando, Royal Marines. 9 October 1944. Age 22.

SALT, Marine, JAMES VALENTINE, PO/X 114584, No. 40 R.M. Commando, Royal Marines. 9 October 1944. Age 20.

ST. ANGE, Marine, WILLIAM JAMES, PO/X 114352, No. 40 R.M. Commando, Royal Marines. 9 October 1944. Age 24.

WHITEHOUSE, Captain, PETER BECKWITH, 100423, Royal Engineers, and No. 2, Commando 9 October 1944. Age 26.

AIR FORCE CASUALTIES

GREEK-ITALIAN CONFLICT, WINTER 1940-41

BROOKS, Sergeant (Pilot) GEORGE NEWCOMBE, 742451, 70 Sqdn., Royal Air Force Volunteer Reserve. 7 November 1940. Age 24.

CHILDS, Sergeant (Pilot) ERIC BORLASE, 566516, 30 Sqdn., Royal Air Force. 15 November 1940. Age 22.

CULLEN, Flight Lieutenant (Pilot) RICHARD NIGEL, 39967, D F C, 80 Sqdn., Royal Air Force. 4 March 1941. Age 23.

ELLAM, Sergeant (W.Op./Air Gnr.) WILFRED, 539774, 70 Sqdn., Royal Air Force. 7 November 1940. Age 23.

MORGAN, Sergeant (Pilot) VICTOR JOHN, 741943, 70 Sqdn., Royal Air Force Volunteer Reserve. 7 November 1940. Age 24.

MURRELL, Sergeant (Pilot) DENNIS CHARLES, 745143, 37 Sqdn., Royal Air Force Volunteer Reserve. 16 March 1941.

NEWMAN, Sergeant (W.Op./Air Gnr.) STANLEY, 811173, 37 Sqdn., Royal Air Force (Auxiliary Air Force). 16 March 1941.

STEWART, Sergeant (Air Gnr.) JOHN GEORGE, 566189, 30 Sqdn., Royal Air Force. 15 November 1940. Age 24.

STOTT, Corporal, DONALD, 526089, 30 Sqdn., Royal Air Force. 15 November 1940. Age 23.

TUBBERDY, Sergeant (W.Op./Air Gnr.) WILLIAM, 538072, 30 Sqdn., Royal Air Force. 18 December 1940. Age 21.

SOE SUPPLY DROP CASUALTIES

BURLEFINGER, Sergeant (W.Op./Air Gnr.) FRANCIS CECIL RUDOLPH, 1317535, 624 Sqdn., Royal Air Force Volunteer Reserve. 1 February 1944. Age 26.

DEVINE, Sergeant (Flt. Engr.) JAMES LEO, 1503292, 624 Sqdn., Royal Air Force Volunteer Reserve. 1 February 1944. Age 22.

GARDNER, Sergeant (Air Gnr.) GEORGE, 2214238, 624 Sqdn., Royal Air Force Volunteer Reserve. 1 February 1944. Age 19.

POTTER, Flight Sergeant (Air Bomber) DENNIS HILTON, 427021, 624 Sqdn., Royal Australian Air Force. 1 February 1944. Age 21.

STANLEY, Flying Officer (Pilot) RONALD EDWIN, 136869, 624 Sqdn., Royal Air Force Volunteer Reserve. 1 February 1944. Age 21.

TENNANT, Flight Sergeant (Pilot) EDWARD DRAKE STEELE, 410105, 624 (R.A.F.) Sqdn., Royal Australian Air Force. 1 February 1944. Age 31.

TURNER, Flight Sergeant (Air Gnr.) DESMOND MAURICE, 1318952, 178 Sqdn., Royal Air Force Volunteer Reserve. 19 March 1944.

WILLIAMS, Flight Sergeant (Air Gnr.) HAROLD, 1576803, 148 Sqdn., Royal Air Force Volunteer Reserve. 20 October 1943. Age 18.

SPITFIRE RECCE RAIDS

DOUGLAS, Flight Lieutenant (Pilot) JOHN GEORGE, 146139, 1435 Sqdn., Royal Air Force Volunteer Reserve. 22 October 1944. Age 26.

WADDELL, Warrant Officer (Pilot) PETER VICTOR, 401163, 249 (R.A.F.) Sqdn., Royal Australian Air Force. 30 March 1944. Age 25.

247

BIBLIOGRAPHY

General History

High Albania – Edith Durham.
    First published in 1909. Also published by Phoenix Press, ISBN 1-84212-207-X

The Burden of the Balkans - Edith Durham
    First Published in 1905. Republished by The Centre for Albanian Studies. ISBN 978-1516996827

Albania and the Albanians (Selected Articles and Letters, 1903-1944) - Edith Durham.
    Published by The Centre for Albanian Studies. ISBN 1 903616-09-3

The London Conference and the Albanian Question – The Despatches of Sir Edward Grey – Edited by Bejtullah Destani and Robert Elsie.
    Published by The Centre for Albanian Studies. ISBN 978-1535304726

Albania – The Master Key to the Near East – Christo Dako.
    First published in 1919. Reprinted by the Institute for Albanian and Protestant Studies. ISBN 978-1-946244-29-1

The Albanians – A Modern History – Miranda Vickers.
    Published by I.B. Taurus, ISBN 1 86064 5410

History of Albania – Tajar Zavalani (Edited by Robert Elsie and Bejtullah Destani)
    Published by Createspace Independent Publishing Platform. ISBN10 1507595670; ISBN13 9781507595671

Albania in Occupation and War - Owen Pearson

Published by The Centre for Albanian Studies. ISBN 1-84511-014-5

Albania As Dictatorship and Democracy - Owen Pearson
Published by The Centre for Albanian Studies. ISBN 1-84511-105-2

Enver Hoxha: The Iron Fist of Albania – Blendi Fevziu
Published by Bloomsbury Publishing PLC. Imprint by I.B. Tauris. ISBN10 1784539708; ISBN13 9781784539702

The Balkans 1804-1999 - Misha Glenny
Published by Granta Books. ISBN 1-86207-073-3

Modern Albania : From Dictatorship to Democracy in Europe – Fred C. Abrahams
Published by New York University Press. ISBN10 1479838098
ISBN13 9781479838097

Archaeology

Albania - An Archaeological Guide - Oliver Gilkes
Published by I.B.Tauris. ISBN 978 1 78076 069 8

New Directions in Albanian Archaeology – Edited by Lorenc Bejko and Richard Hodges
Published by International Center for Albanian Archaeology. ISBN 99943-923-0-1

Religion

A Dictionary of Albanian Religion, Mythology and Folk Culture – Robert Elsie
Published by Hurst & Company, London. ISBN 1-85065-570-7

The Albanian Bektashi: History and Culture of a Dervish Order in the Balkans – Robert Elsie.
Published by Bloomsbury Publishing. ISBN 9781788315715

Literature

Classical Albanian Literature - A Reader - Robert Elsie
Published by The Centre for Albanian Studies. ISBN 978-1515132769

Albanian Literature: A Short History – Robert Elsie.
Published by I. B. Tauris. ISBN 1-84511-031-5

History of Albanian Literature – Volume One and Volume Two – Robert Elsie
Published by Social Science Monographs, Boulder. ISBN 0-88033-276-X

Albanian Literature - S.E. Mann
Published by Bernard Quaritch Ltd in 1955

Under The Banners of Melancholy – Collected Works of Migjeni – Migjeni. Translated by Robert Elsie.
Published by The Centre for Albanian Studies. ISBN 978-1508675990

World War Two – British Involvement

Albanian Assignment - David Smiley
Published by Chatto & Windus - The Hogarth Press. ISBN 0 7011 2869 0

Sons of the Eagle - Julian Amery
Published by Hailer Publishing. ISBN 0-9767380-5-8

The Wildest Province - SOE in the Land of the Eagle - Roderick Bailey

Published by Vintage Books. ISBN 9781845950712

King Zog

Albania and King Zog - Owen Pearson.
Published by The Centre for Albanian Studies. ISBN 1-84511-013-7

King Zog – Self-Made Monarch of Albania – Jason Tomes.
Published by Sutton Publishing. ISBN 0-7509-3077-2

Geraldine of the Albanians – Gwen Robyns.
Published by Anchor Brendon Ltd. ISBN 0-58411133-9

Ten Years, Ten Months, Ten Days – Antoinette De Szinyei-Merse.
Originally published in Hungarian. Translated by Dr Paul Tabori. English edition published by Hutchinson & Co in 1940, and 150 copies reprinted by Royalty Digest.

A Royal Exile. King Zog and Queen Geraldine of Albania – Neil Rees.
Published by Neil Rees, Studge Publications. ISBN 978-0-9550883-1-5

Scanderbeg

Scanderbeg, The Hero of Europe – Three Books – Shpetim Lezi.
ISBN 9781505644685

Scanderbeg – Harry Hodgkinson
Published by The Centre for Albanian Studies. ISBN 1-873928130

General Travel Guide

Albania – Gillian Gloyer.

Published by Bradt Travel Guides (2018). ISBN10 1784770787; ISBN13 9781784770785

Other

Kanuni i Lekë Dukhagjinit. Translated by Leonard Fox.
Published by Gjonlekaj Publishing Company. ISBN 0-9622141-0-8

The Hasluck Collection of Albanian Folktales – Margaret Hasluck. Edited by Robert Elsie.
Published by The Centre for Albanian Studies. ISBN 978-1512002287

Albanian Folktales and Legends – Robert Elsie.
Published by The Centre for Albanian Studies. ISBN 978-1507631300

www.ingramcontent.com/pod-product-compliance
Lightning Source LLC
LaVergne TN
LVHW010504200726
843506LV00013B/2519